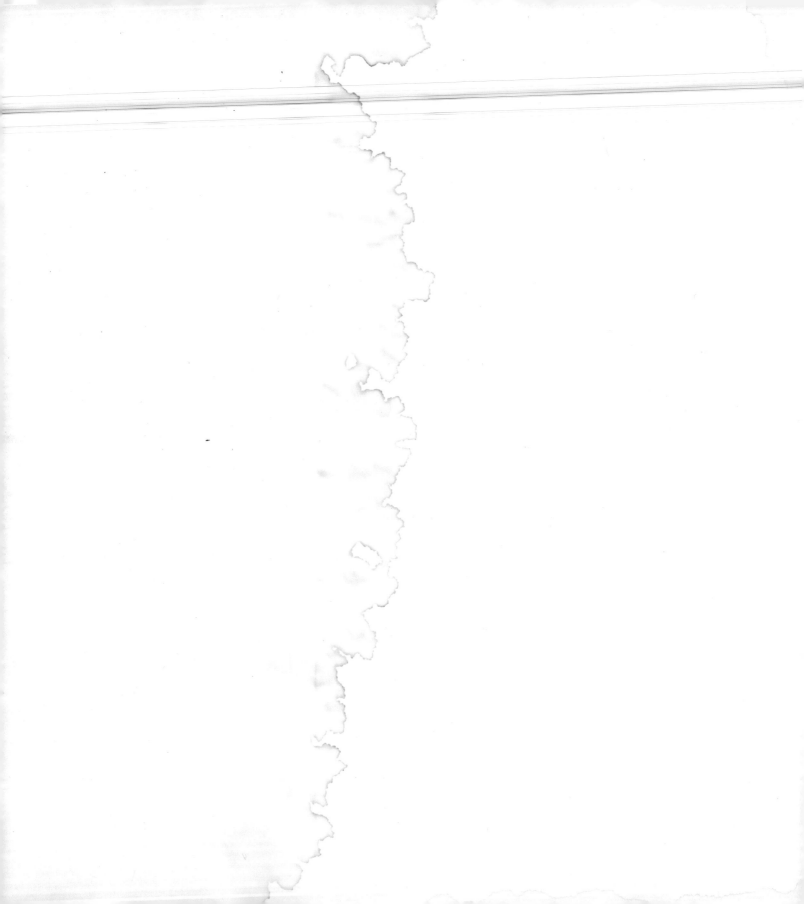

To my mother

Please note the following:

Quantities given in all the recipes serve 4 people unless otherwise stated.

Butter and margarine are packaged in a variety of forms, including 1-pound blocks and ¼-pound sticks. A stick equals 8 tablespoons (½ cup).

Cream used is specified as light cream (containing from 18 percent to 30 percent milk fat), whipping cream (30 percent to 36 percent milk fat), or heavy cream (at least 36 percent milk fat).

Flour used is all-purpose flour, unless otherwise specified.

Preparation of ingredients, such as the cleaning, trimming, and peeling of vegetables and fruit, is presumed and the text refers to any aspect of this only if unusual, such as onions used unpeeled, etc.

Citrus fruit should be thoroughly washed to remove any agricultural residues. For this reason, whenever a recipe uses the rind of any citrus such as oranges, lemon, or limes, the text specifies washed fruit. Wash the fruit thoroughly, rinse well, and pat dry. If using organically grown fruit, rinse briefly and pat dry.

Eggs used are large unless otherwise specified. Because of the risk of contamination with salmonella bacteria, current recommendations from health professionals are that children, pregnant women, people on immuno-suppressant drugs, and the elderly should not eat raw or lightly cooked eggs. This book includes recipes with raw and lightly cooked eggs. These recipes are marked by an ★ in the text.

Editorial Direction: Lewis Esson Publishing
Art Direction: Mary Evans
Design: Sue Storey
Illustrations: Allison Barratt
Food for Photography: Jane Suthering
Styling: Roisin Nield
Editorial Assistant: Penny David
American Editor: Norma MacMillan
Production: Alison McIver

Published by Cole Group
4415 Sonoma Highway/PO Box 4089
Santa Rosa, CA 95402-4089
(707) 538-0492   FAX (707) 538-0497

First published in 1993 by
Conran Octopus Limited.
37 Shelton Street, London WC2H 9HN

A   B   C   D   E   F   G   H
3   4   5   6   7   8   9   0

ISBN 1-56426-655-9

Library of Congress Cataloguing in process
Typeset by Servis Filmsetting Ltd
Printed and bound in Hong Kong by Mandarin Offset

Distributed to the book trade by Publishers Group West

THE CREATIVE COOK

Classic Cakes

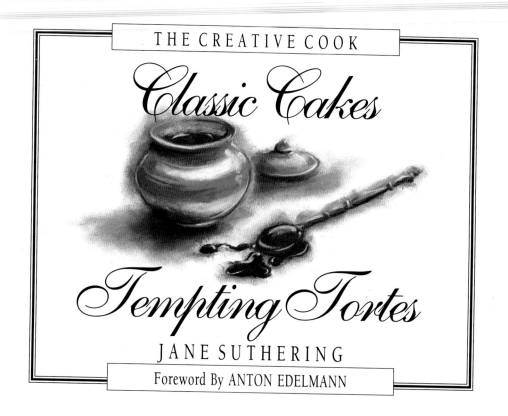

Tempting Tortes

JANE SUTHERING

Foreword By ANTON EDELMANN

COLE
GROUP

CONTENTS

FOREWORD

I imagine that most people think of the work of a chef at a large hotel as principally revolving around lunches and dinners. However, at the Savoy we also put a great deal of thought and effort into the service of morning coffee and afternoon tea. For these, we are able to bring to bear our skills in *pâtisserie*, an area in which most chefs did their early training and which is a great creative challenge as well as always being fun to return to.

The cakes in Jane's book exemplify my own attitude toward cake-making. She takes the traditional cakes from any cuisines, such as Viennese Griestorte and Spanish Olive Oil and Sweet Wine Cake, and gives them her very own special interpretation – always to memorable and satisfying effect.

Jane's philosophy is also that anyone can make good cakes if they simply read their recipes carefully, prepare ahead properly, and exercise a little care. Throughout this book she gives such clear and uncomplicated instructions that it is almost impossible not to produce wonderful results every time.

So, if you want to enjoy an elegant afternoon tea at home, create a splendid torte to give a finishing flourish to your next dinner party, or simply have something nice in the pantry for coffee in the morning, dip into this book and enjoy every last crumb.

ANTON EDELMANN

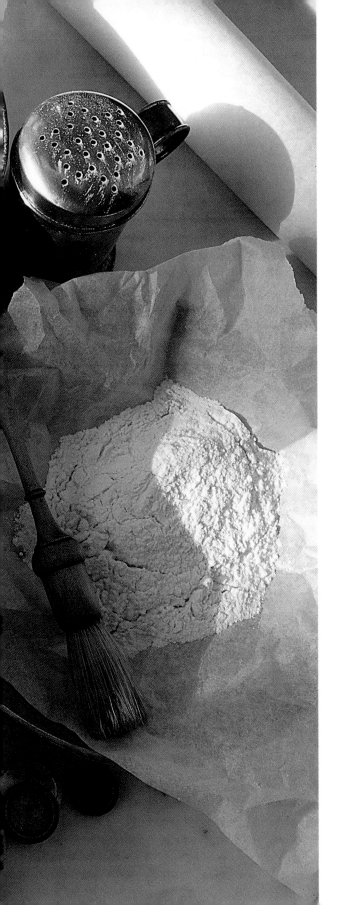

INTRODUCTION

I often hear people say that they "can't make cakes," but I think that this is generally nonsense. With a tried and tested recipe to follow, some time to spare, and a little patience, the rewarding art of baking can soon be mastered.

Admittedly, certain rules must be followed to achieve a good cake, and after years of trial and error in my quest for perfect cakes, it is my wish to relay these to you in the easiest possible way.

- Start by reading the recipes from beginning to end.
- Measure all the ingredients and do basic preparation, such as grating, before you start cooking.
- Basic ingredients such as butter, sugar, eggs, and flour combine better together when they are at room temperature. Butter may need softening further, but do not let it become oily.

Mixtures that are "creamed" (which means beating the butter and sugar together) must be worked for a long time until the mixture is almost white (if using granulated sugar) or pale and fluffy (if using a brown sugar) and have a "soft dropping consistency" (the mixture will fall off the spoon or beaters easily when tapped on the edge of the bowl).

Mixtures that are "beaten" (which means beating the eggs and sugar together) must be beaten until thick and mousse-like; the beaters should easily leave a trail in the mixture when they are removed. To aid beating, the bowl is sometimes set over a saucepan of simmering water, as this helps to stabilize the mixture. (Obviously, with a large countertop mixer no heat is used – nor is it needed.) Beating will take about 8 minutes with a hand mixer.

- When adding eggs to a creamed mixture, add them one by one. Better still, beat the eggs and add the beaten egg little by little, beating it very well between each addition so that the egg is fully incorporated into the creamed mixture before the next amount is added. If, by any chance, the mixture does start to curdle, you can rectify this by beating in a spoonful of the measured flour.
- "Folding in" is achieved by using a large metal spoon or rubber spatula and working in a figure-eight movement. It is one of the oddities of life that some of the flour will always stay in a clump on the spoon, so check it toward the end of mixing.
- Do not leave a beaten batter to stand once it is made – put it straight in the oven.
- When beating egg whites, make sure that the bowl and beaters are scrupulously clean. Start beating, then add a pinch of salt or a squeeze of lemon juice to help stabilize the mixture.
- If adding dried fruit and alcohol to a cake, macerate them together at least 1 hour before baking, or even up to 1 week ahead. The fruit will absorb the alcohol and stay moister in the cake.

- Moist mixtures that are to be combined should be of a similar consistency. If you want to incorporate beaten egg whites into a firmer mixture, start by adding a little of the egg white to that mixture to "loosen" it and give it a consistency more like that of the egg whites.
- Cake batters will generally find their own levels as they bake. However, it is a good idea to spread a cake batter evenly in the pan, especially if it has a topping sprinkled over the surface. If making a cake in a loaf pan, make a dip along the length of a creamed batter because it tends to peak easily. For some cakes it is nice to have a slightly peaked center, but if you want a completely flat surface for frosting then make a slight dip in the center of the batter before baking.
- Don't open the oven door in the early stages of baking – it can cause a cake to sink!
- If a cake is browning too quickly during baking, cover the top with wax paper or foil.
- To test if a cake is cooked, press the surface lightly with your fingertips – it should be springy to the touch. If you're unsure, insert a fine metal skewer in the center of the cake – it will come out clean if the cake is cooked and it will be piping hot to the touch. The best temperature gauge is your lip, but do proceed with extreme caution!
- Leave cakes in their pans until the pan is cool enough to handle, then carefully unmold and transfer to a wire rack. To keep a moist texture, invert the pan back over the cake until it is cold.

CHOOSING AND USING PANS

In my experience, it is false economy to buy cheap pans. Wherever possible buy top grade cake pans – they will last a lifetime. Cheap ones tend to be thin and often get misshapen in the oven. They also have a tendency to discolor or rust.

To bake most cakes, you will need four 8-inch layer cake pans, a 9-×5-×3-inch loaf pan, a range of springform cake pans, from 8-inch to 10-inch diameters, and an 8-inch square pan.

- Nonstick surfaces are particularly useful in springform pans, loaf pans and baking sheets. If you don't have nonstick surfaces, then use parchment paper or wax paper to line the pans. Some may need to be lined in the bottom only, while others need bottom and side lining.

Parchment cake-pan liners are available. These are made to fit 8- and 9-inch round pans, and look like giant cupcake-pan liners.

For mixtures that have a tendency to stick, such as meringue disks, it's a good idea to use nonstick silicone paper for lining pans.

- When preparing pans for sponge cakes grease them with melted butter and line the bottom with wax or parchment paper, then sprinkle the sides of the pan with an equal quantity of sugar and flour and shake out the excess. This will give the sides of the cake a nice sugary finish.
- To stop a rich fruitcake from being over-baked at the bottom and sides, grease the pan with melted butter, line the bottom and sides with a double thickness of wax or parchment paper, and wrap the outside of the pan with a thick layer of brown paper or newspaper. Sit the pan on thick paper as well.
- Prepare the pans before you start cooking.
- Set the pan directly on the oven rack and never on a baking sheet unless stipulated in the recipe. Setting it on a baking sheet will produce a darker bottom.
- Always clean your pans carefully and dry them thoroughly, preferably in the oven.

CHOOSING AND USING INGREDIENTS
Fats and oils:
I use *butter* most of the time for my cakes. I prefer the natural taste and think the flavor of the finished cake is better. If you are making a strong-flavored cake such as gingerbread or chocolate, however, a good-quality *margarine* will suffice.

Oil or melted butter is used in some recipes to enrich and soften the texture of the cake. If making a nut cake, it is nice to add the appropriate *nut oil*; otherwise a *light vegetable oil*, such as sunflower or peanut, is appropriate. In some special instances an *olive oil* may be appropriate.

Unsalted butter is recommended for frostings.

Sugars:
Granulated sugar is the most popular sugar to use in cakes. *Superfine sugar* is sometimes called for because it dissolves more readily.

Brown sugar has molasses added for flavor. It may be dark brown or light brown, according to the quantity of molasses added. Make sure there are no lumps in the sugar before use.

Most sugars can be used interchangeably in a cake recipe, but the texture and flavor of the finished cake will be altered to some extent.

Flours:
A "soft" flour with a low gluten content is best for cakes. Gluten is the protein that gives flour its strength and helps determine the texture of a finished cake. Any dense flour should be sifted once – or even twice – to lighten it and eliminate lumps.

All-purpose flour, a blend of hard and soft wheats, is fine for most cakes. Finely milled, soft-wheat *cake flour* should be used for lighter, more tender cakes.

Self-rising flour is usually cake flour with added baking powder and sometimes salt.

Baking powder can be added to *all-purpose flour or cake flour* for use instead of self-rising flour – usually 2½ teaspoons to every 1⅔ cups flour for a creamed method cake.

Whole wheat flour does tend to be denser, so extra baking powder may be added to lighten the finished cake. Or, you can use half white and half whole wheat flour to give a "nuttier" flavor. Do not sift whole wheat flour as this extracts all the bran.

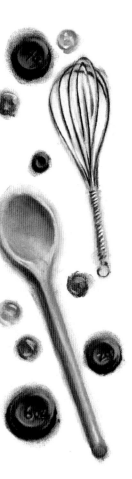

SMALL CAKES AND SCONES

There is something particularly attractive about food in miniature, and small cakes are no exception. They look pretty, are often easier to make and quicker to cook than large cakes, and, in general, they usually store well. Some – like scones, rock buns, doughnuts, and griddle cakes – are, however, far better eaten when freshly made, having had time only to cool to the perfect temperature for eating.

All sorts of wonderful miniature pans are now available from specialty kitchenware stores or gourmet shops to help produce prettily shaped small cakes without much effort. Always grease small pans well and let the cakes cool in them.

Clockwise from the top: Apricot Doughnuts (page 12), Helen's Molasses Griddle Cakes (page 12) and Rum Babas (page 13)

RUM BABAS *are said to owe their origin to King Stanislas of Poland who, while exiled in France, had his chef soak his yeast cake in rum. Legend also has it that he named it after the hero of his favorite story – Ali Baba. Normally, babas are baked in special thimble-shaped molds, but individual savarin rings and brioche molds can also be used.*

HELEN'S MOLASSES GRIDDLE CAKES

MAKES ABOUT 16

1 cup self-rising flour
pinch salt
3 1/2 tbsp sugar
1 egg
2 1/2 tbsp dark molasses
5 tbsp milk
1 1/2 tsp baking powder
butter, for frying and serving

Sift the flour and salt into a bowl and stir in the sugar. Mix in the egg, molasses, and milk to produce a thick batter.

Beat 2 minutes with a wooden spoon until smooth. Add the baking powder and beat 30 seconds longer. Let rest 5 minutes while warming a griddle or frying pan over low heat.

Brush the warm griddle or pan with butter and drop tablespoonfuls of the batter spaced well apart on it. Cook about 2 minutes on each side, turning occasionally, until golden brown and just springy to the touch.

Remove from the griddle or pan and keep warm, wrapped in a clean dish towel. Continue making griddle cakes in the same way until all the batter is used. Serve spread with butter.

APRICOT DOUGHNUTS

MAKES 16

3 cups flour
4 1/2 tbsp sugar, plus more for coating
1/2 tsp salt
2 cakes fresh yeast or 2 packages active dry yeast
1 1/4 cups lukewarm milk
2 tbsp apricot liqueur or apricot brandy
3/4 cup chopped dried apricots
1/3 cup apricot preserves
vegetable oil, for deep-frying

Sift the flour, sugar, and salt into a large bowl and make a well in the center.

In a small bowl, mix the yeast with a little of the milk, then gradually add the remaining milk. Pour this into the well and cover with a little of the flour. Cover and let proof about 10 minutes, until the yeast mixture is frothy.

Add the oil, eggs, and liqueur and beat well until light in texture. Beat in the apricots. Cover and let rise in a warm place until about doubled in size.

Turn the dough onto a floured surface and cut it into 16 pieces. One at a time, knead the pieces lightly, then flatten them out with your hand and place a teaspoonful of preserves in the center. Draw the dough around the preserves and seal it carefully.

Set the doughnuts well apart on floured baking sheets. Cover and let rise until about doubled in size (the dough should spring back when pressed).

Heat the oil to 360°F (a small cube of dry bread browns in 60 seconds) and fry the doughnuts in batches of 4, until golden brown and cooked through, about 4 minutes on each side.

Drain thoroughly, then immediately toss in sugar. Serve as soon as all are cooked.

RUM BABAS

MAKES 8

2 tbsp dark rum
⅓ cup raisins
⅓ cup dried currants
1 stick (8 tbsp) butter, melted, plus more for greasing
1 package quick-rise dry yeast
1⅔ cups flour
4½ tbsp sugar
4 eggs, beaten
FOR THE SYRUP
¾ cup sugar
5 tbsp dark rum

Mix the 2 tablespoons of rum and the dried fruit in a bowl, cover, and let soak at least 1 hour or up to 24 hours.

Grease 8 large (about ⅔ cup) individual brioche molds with butter.

Mix the yeast, flour, and sugar in a large bowl. Beat in the butter and eggs until the batter is light in texture. Beat in the fruit and rum.

Half-fill the molds with the batter, then cover and let rise in a warm place until the batter reaches the top of the molds.

Preheat the oven to 400°F.

Bake the babas until golden brown and just firm to the touch, 15–20 minutes. Let cool a little, then unmold into a shallow dish.

Make the syrup: In a small saucepan set over medium heat, dissolve the sugar in ⅞ cup of water. Once the sugar is completely dissolved, bring to a simmer and simmer 5 minutes. Stir in the rum and remove from the heat.

Immediately pour the hot syrup over the babas and leave until they have absorbed all the syrup.

MOIST CHOCOLATE SQUARES

MAKES 9

5 tbsp butter, softened, plus more for greasing
4 oz semi sweet chocolate, broken into pieces
3 eggs, separated
¾ cup ground almonds
½ cup+2 tbsp confectioners' sugar, sifted
1 tbsp flour, sifted
pinch of salt
unsweetened cocoa powder, for dusting
confectioners' sugar, for dusting

Preheat the oven to 350°F. Grease a 7½-inch square cake pan with butter and line the bottom with wax or parchment paper.

In a small bowl, melt the chocolate with 2 tablespoons of water, either in a microwave oven or set over a saucepan of simmering water.

Remove from the heat and beat in the butter until evenly incorporated. Beat in the egg yolks one at a time. Then stir in the ground almonds, confectioners' sugar, and flour.

Beat the egg whites with a pinch of salt until stiff. Then carefully fold into the chocolate mixture.

Transfer to the prepared pan and bake until risen and just firm to the touch, about 20 minutes.

Let cool in the pan. Trim the edges, if necessary, and then cut into 9 squares. Dust with cocoa powder and confectioners' sugar.

SANDCASTLES

MAKES 8

1 ½ sticks (¾ cup) butter, melted, plus more for greasing
1 cup sugar
3 eggs
¼ tsp pure vanilla extract
finely grated zest of ½ washed lemon
1 cup self-rising flour
1 cup cornstarch
pinch of salt

Preheat the oven to 325°F. Grease 8 miniature loaf pans with butter, then line their bottoms with wax or parchment paper.

Reserve 4 teaspoons of the sugar. In a large bowl set over simmering water, beat the eggs, remaining sugar, and flavorings until thick and pale.

Sift the flour, cornstarch, and salt together and fold them into the beaten mixture in 2 batches. Then mix in the butter in 2 batches until thoroughly incorporated.

Divide the batter among the prepared pans. Then sprinkle the surface of each one with ½ teaspoon of the reserved sugar.

Bake until risen and golden and just firm to the touch, about 25 minutes. Cool slightly, then un-mold onto wire racks. Serve plain or with preserves.

ECCLES CAKE

MAKES 12

2 tbsp butter, plus more for greasing
¾ lb puff pastry
¾ cup dried currants
3 tbsp diced mixed candied peel
3 tbsp light brown sugar
½ tsp apple pie spice
granulated sugar, for sprinkling

Preheat the oven to 425°F and grease a baking sheet with butter.

On a lightly floured surface, roll out the pastry thinly. Using a 4-inch cookie cutter, stamp out 12 rounds.

In a bowl, combine the currants, peel, brown sugar, and spice. Spoon a little of this mixture into the center of each pastry round.

Dampen the edges of the pastry with water and pull them up all around so that they meet in the middle. Pinch well to seal.

Turn each pastry over and press down with the flat of your hand until the filling is clearly visible.

Make a couple of slashes in the top of each pastry, brush them lightly with water, and sprinkle with granulated sugar.

Bake until crisp and golden, 15–20 minutes. Let cool on a wire rack.

Left to right: Eccles Cakes, Moist Chocolate Squares (page 13), and Sandcastles

COCONUT AND CHERRY MACAROONS

MAKES 10

2 egg whites
¾ cup confectioners' sugar, sifted
1¼ cups dried shredded coconut
1⅓ cups ground almonds
⅓ cup chopped candied cherries
1 tbsp dark rum or dry sherry wine

Preheat the oven to 300°F and line a baking sheet with nonstick silicone paper.

Combine all the ingredients in a bowl and then shape the mixture into 10 round cakes.

Place these on the baking sheet. Bake until lightly golden, about 20 minutes.

Let cool on a wire rack.

FUDGE BROWNIES

MAKES 9

6 tbsp butter, diced, plus more for greasing
3 oz best-quality white chocolate, broken into pieces
2 eggs
½ tsp pure vanilla extract
¼ tsp salt
1¼ cups light brown sugar
¾ cup self-rising flour
1 cup chopped walnuts

Preheat the oven to 350°F. Grease an 8-inch square pan with butter and line the bottom with wax or parchment paper.

Place the chocolate and butter in a bowl set over simmering water and heat gently until they have just melted.

Beat the eggs, vanilla, salt, and sugar together in another bowl until thickened. Then stir in the flour and melted chocolate mixture, followed by the walnuts.

Transfer the batter to the prepared pan. Bake until risen and just firm to the touch, about 30 minutes. Let cool in the pan and then cut into 9 square pieces.

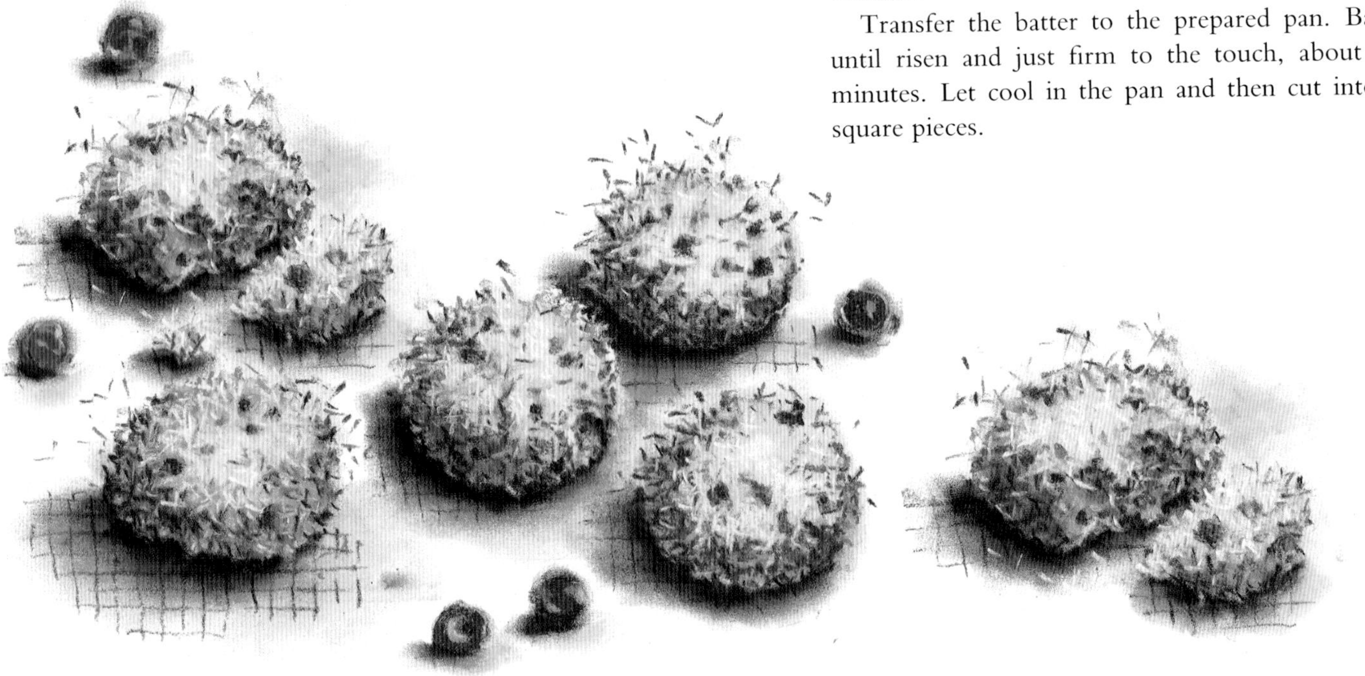

CURTSY TARTS

MAKES ABOUT 15

2 ½ cups milk
4 ½ tbsp sugar
2 tsp rennet
3 tbsp butter, softened
1 egg
⅓ cup ground almonds
1 tbsp brandy
6 oz puff pastry
about 5 tbsp raspberry preserves

In a small saucepan, gently warm the milk with half the sugar until just lukewarm (you should be able to dip your little finger into it). Stir in the rennet and set aside for about 30 minutes until it starts to set.

Line a strainer with cheesecloth and spoon in the mixture. Cover and set over a bowl to drip overnight. Discard the liquid in the bowl, but reserve the curds left in the strainer.

Preheat the oven to 425°F.

In a bowl, beat the butter with the remaining sugar and the curds until smooth. Then beat in the egg, ground almonds, and brandy.

On a lightly floured surface, roll out the pastry thinly and use it to line about 15 shallow muffin tins or tartlet molds. Prick the pastry shells with a fork. Spoon a little jam into each one, then top with the curd mixture and spread in to the edges.

Bake until risen and golden, 20–25 minutes.

Let cool on a wire rack, but serve freshly baked.

CARAWAY FLUTES

MAKES 12

6 tbsp butter, softened, plus more for greasing
4 ½ tbsp sugar
2 eggs, beaten
2 tbsp marmalade
1 cup self-rising flour, sifted
pinch of salt
1 tsp caraway seeds

Preheat the oven to 325°F and grease 12 fluted molds about 2¾-inches wide and 1¼-inches deep (about 3 tablespoons capacity) with butter.

Cream the butter and sugar together in a bowl until almost white. Beat in the eggs a little at a time, then stir in the marmalade. Finally, fold in the flour, salt, and caraway seeds.

Divide the batter among the prepared molds and bake until risen and golden and just firm to the touch, about 15 minutes.

Let cool slightly, then unmold on a wire rack. If desired, glaze with a little more warmed marmalade.

CURTSY TARTS are a variation of classic Maids of Honor, said to have been created by Anne Boleyn for Henry VIII while she was still lady-in-waiting to Catherine of Aragon. They are called "curtsy" because they dip down as they come out of the oven.

RENNET, an animal extract that contains an enzyme, encourages milk to set. Vegetarian rennet, made from plants, is also available.

SULTANA SCONES

MAKES 10

4 tbsp butter, diced, plus more for greasing
2 cups self-rising flour
pinch of salt
pinch of freshly grated nutmeg
2 tbsp sugar
⅓ cup golden raisins (sultanas)
½ cup milk

Preheat the oven to 425°F and grease a baking sheet with butter.

Sift the flour, salt and nutmeg into a bowl. Then rub in the butter until the mixture resembles fine crumbs.

Stir in the sugar and raisins. Then mix to a firm dough with the milk.

On a lightly floured surface, roll out the dough to a thickness of about ¾ inch. Using a cookie cutter or the rim of a glass, stamp out ten 2½-inch rounds, re-rolling the trimmings as necessary.

Transfer the rounds to the prepared baking sheet and bake until well-risen and golden, 15–20 minutes.

Serve as soon as possible, with butter or whipped or clotted cream and preserves.

ROCK BUNS

MAKES 8

6 tbsp butter, diced, plus more for greasing
1½ cups flour (or equal parts white flour and whole wheat flour)
2 tbsp rice flour
2 tsp baking powder
pinch of salt
7 tbsp sugar
⅔ cup mixed dried fruit
1 egg
2 tbsp milk

Preheat the oven to 400°F and grease a baking sheet with butter.

Mix the flour(s), rice flour, baking powder, and salt together in a large bowl. Rub in the butter until the mixture resembles fine crumbs, then stir in the sugar and fruit.

Beat the egg and milk together and add this to the mixture to give a stiff dough.

Spoon 8 mounds of the mixture well apart on the the baking sheet and bake until golden and firm to the touch, 15–20 minutes.

Let cool on a wire rack.

Left: Sultana Scones; right: Rock Buns

Both Sultana Scones *and* Rock Buns *are ideal for serving fresh from the oven to impress unexpected guests. The rubbed-in mixture can be kept in a plastic bag in the refrigerator or freezer and the liquid ingredients added just before shaping and baking.*

QUICK AND EASY CAKES

The cakes in this chapter are for all those many occasions when you wish you had a piece of cake to offer a friend with mid-morning coffee or a cup of tea in the afternoon, or when you realize too late that you forgot to make a dessert.

The baked cakes rely on soft tub margarine or shortening to speed up the mixing process. The basic ingredients are all beaten together in a bowl for a minute or two only. Then the flavorings are added as the batter is in the oven as quick as a flash.

The other speedy way to make a cake is like that used for Chocolate Refrigerator Cake, which doesn't need baking at all, but sets when chilled. You do have to plan such cakes ahead, however, as the chilling takes time.

Left: Mascarpone and Raspberry Dessert Cake (page 22); right: Chocolate Refrigerator Cake (page 23)

MASCARPONE AND RASPBERRY DESSERT CAKE

SERVES 8–12

32 ladyfingers
½ cup Marsala wine
1 ½ cups raspberries, thawed if frozen
3 oz Amaretti cookies, crushed
unsweetened cocoa powder, for dusting
FOR THE MASCARPONE CREAM
3 ½ tbsp custard powder or cornstarch
2 egg yolks
1 ¼ cups milk
1 ¼ cups confectioners' sugar, sifted
1 lb 2 oz mascarpone cheese

First start making the mascarpone cream: In a large bowl, mix the custard powder and egg yolks with a little of the milk. Heat the remaining milk with a little of the sugar to just below boiling point and pour this over the custard. Return this mixture to the pan and cook, stirring constantly, until thickened. Transfer to a bowl, cover, and let cool.

Meanwhile, line the bottom and sides of an 8¾-inch springform cake pan with nonstick silicone paper.

Finish the mascarpone cream by beating the cheese with the rest of the sugar. Beat this into the cold custard until smooth and light in texture.

Set 16 ladyfingers in the bottom of the prepared pan and sprinkle over half the Marsala. Spread with half the mascarpone cream, then sprinkle the raspberries on top. Repeat the layers of ladyfingers and mascarpone cream.

Cover the cake with a round of parchment and chill at least 8 hours, but preferably overnight.

Set the cake on a plate. Remove the sides of the pan. Turn the cake upside down on another plate and remove the base and base paper. Turn the bake back the right way up on the serving plate. Remove the top and side papers. Smooth the top and sides.

Press some of the crushed Amaretti cookies on the sides to cover them and sprinkle the rest on top of the cake. Chill until required.

Dust heavily with cocoa powder just before serving.

GREAT GRAPEFRUIT CAKE

SERVES 8–12

½ cup soft tub margarine
½ cup + 2 tbsp granulated sugar
2 eggs
1 ½ cups self-rising flour
½ tsp baking powder
pinch of salt
finely grated zest of 1 washed grapefruit
juice of 2 grapefruit
½ cup confectioners' sugar
butter or vegetable oil, for greasing

Preheat the oven to 350°F. Grease an 8-inch square pan with butter or oil and line the bottom with wax or parchment paper.

Place the margarine, granulated sugar, eggs, flour, baking powder, salt, and grapefruit zest in a large bowl and beat well with a wooden spoon for 1–2 minutes, until the mixture has a "soft dropping consistency." Transfer to the prepared pan and level the surface of the batter. Bake until risen and just firm to the touch, about 30 minutes. Let cool in the pan.

Place the grapefruit juice and confectioners' sugar in a saucepan and bring to a boil. Boil until slightly syrupy, about 3–4 minutes. Prick the top of the cake all over with a skewer and pour the syrup over it. Let cool completely in the pan.

Unmold the cake and cut it into fingers. Dust with extra confectioners' sugar, if desired.

CHOCOLATE REFRIGERATOR CAKE★

SERVES 12

½ cup walnut pieces
½ cup blanched almonds
⅓ cup golden raisins (sultanas)
⅓ cup chopped candied cherries
2 cups graham-cracker crumbs, firmly packed
5 oz semisweet chocolate, melted
1 extra large egg, beaten
(★see page 2 for advice on eggs)
3–4 tbsp dark rum, or more to taste
FOR DECORATION (OPTIONAL)
whipped cream
2 maraschino or candied cherries, cut into thin wedges

Preheat the oven to 350°F and line an 8-inch tart pan with foil. Place the nuts on a baking sheet and toast them in oven until golden, about 20 minutes.

Roughly chop the toasted nuts and combine them with the fruit and graham-cracker crumbs in a large bowl. Stir in the chocolate. Add the egg and 3–4 tablespoons rum. Check the taste and add a little more rum, if desired.

Press the mixture into the prepared pan and chill at least 4 hours or preferably overnight.

Unmold the chilled cake and cut into 12 wedges. If desired, top each wedge with a swirl of whipped cream and a piece of cherry.

MINCEMEAT CAKE

SERVES 8

½ cup soft tub margarine
⅔ cup light brown sugar
2 eggs
¾ cup self-rising flour
½ cup whole wheat self-rising flour
½ tsp baking powder
1 tbsp warm water
1 cup mincemeat
butter or vegetable oil, for greasing
FOR THE ICING
1 ½ cups confectioners sugar, sifted
2 tbsp tangerine juice

Preheat the oven to 325°F. Grease an 8-inch round cake pan with butter or oil and line the bottom with wax or parchment paper.

In a large bowl, combine all the ingredients for the cake and beat well with a wooden spoon for about 2 minutes, until the batter has a "soft dropping consistency." Transfer to the prepared pan and level the surface.

Bake until risen and just firm to the touch, about 40 minutes. Let cool in the pan and then transfer to a wire rack to cool completely.

Make the icing by mixing the confectioners' sugar with the juice until smooth. Spread this over the top of the cake. Let it set.

Toasting the nuts before adding them to the CHOCOLATE REFRIGERATOR CAKE *adds an extra depth of flavor. If desired, replace the almonds and walnuts with an equal quantity of other nuts such as pecans, hazelnuts, brazils, or macadamia nuts.*

MINCEMEAT CAKE *is a clever way of using up mincemeat left over after the holidays.*

VERY GINGERBREAD WITH LEMON ICING

SERVES 9–16

1 stick (8 tbsp) butter, plus more for greasing
¾ cup + 2 tbsp all-purpose flour
pinch of salt
1 tsp apple pie spice
1 tbsp ground ginger
¾ cup + 2 tbsp whole wheat flour
5 tbsp raw brown sugar
⅓ cup chopped preserved stem ginger
⅓ cup dark molasses
⅓ cup light corn syrup
1 tsp baking soda
½ cup warm milk
1 extra large egg, beaten
FOR THE LEMON ICING
½ cup confectioners' sugar, sifted
2 ½ tsp lemon juice

Preheat the oven to 350°F. Grease an 8-inch square cake pan with butter and line the bottom with wax or parchment paper.

Sift the all-purpose flour, salt, and spices into a large bowl, then stir in the whole wheat flour, brown sugar, and chopped ginger.

In a saucepan, warm the butter, molasses, and corn syrup together until the butter just melts.

Dissolve the baking soda in the milk and add this to the dry ingredients together with the syrup mixture and egg. Beat the batter well until smooth.

Transfer to the pan and bake until risen and firm to the touch, 40–45 minutes. Cool slightly in the pan, then unmold and cool completely on a rack.

Make the icing: Mix the confectioners' sugar and lemon juice in a bowl until thick and smooth. Drizzle this over the cake in a random pattern and let set. Cut into squares to serve.

WARM CINNAMON CAKE

SERVES 8–10

1 ⅔ cups flour
1 tbsp baking powder
½ tsp salt
½ cup + 2 tbsp sugar
½ cup shortening or soft tub margarine
1 egg
6 tbsp milk
butter, for greasing
vanilla ice-cream, for serving (optional)
FOR THE TOPPING
3 tbsp flour
3 tbsp sugar
1 tbsp ground cinnamon
3 tbsp shortening or soft tub margarine

Preheat the oven to 400°F. Grease a 10-inch round cake pan with butter and line the bottom with wax or parchment paper.

First, make the topping by sifting the dry ingredients together and rubbing in the fat.

Then make the cake: Sift the dry ingredients into a bowl and add the shortening, egg, and milk. Beat 1 minute with a wooden spoon until smooth and then transfer to the prepared pan.

Sprinkle evenly with the topping and bake until well risen, about 25 minutes (don't be tempted to press it with your finger to check if it's cooked – the sugar in the topping will be very hot!).

Serve straight from the oven, plain or with vanilla ice-cream.

Left: Very Gingerbread with Lemon Icing; right: Warm Cinnamon Cake

ESPRESSO COFFEE GRANULES *are freeze-dried to give a more authentic coffee taste. Available from most supermarkets, they are very useful for adding a good flavor to cakes and frostings. Always dissolve them in a little boiling water before use.*

ONE-STEP COFFEE LAYER CAKE

SERVES 8

¾ cup soft tub margarine
¾ cup+2 tbsp sugar
3 eggs
1½ cups self-rising flour
1 tsp baking powder
pinch of salt
1 tbsp espresso coffee granules, dissolved in 1 tbsp boiling water
butter or vegetable oil, for greasing
candied coffee beans, for decoration

FOR THE FILLING

6 tbsp butter, softened
1 tbsp espresso coffee granules, dissolved in 1 tbsp boiling water
1½ cups confectioners' sugar, sifted

FOR THE ICING

¾ cup confectioners' sugar, sifted
1½ tsp espresso coffee granules, dissolved in 2½ tsp boiling water

Preheat the oven to 350°F. Grease two 8-inch layer cake pans with butter or oil and line the bottoms with wax or parchment paper.

Place all the ingredients for the cake in a large bowl and beat well with a wooden spoon for 1–2 minutes until mixed to a "soft dropping consistency."

Divide the batter between the pans and bake until risen and just firm to the touch, about 25 minutes. Let cool slightly in the pans, then transfer to wire racks and let cool completely.

Make the filling: Beat the butter in a bowl until soft and almost white, then stir in the coffee solution and beat in the confectioners' sugar. Use two-thirds of this mixture to put the cake layers together.

Make the icing: Mix the confectioners' sugar and coffee solution until smooth and then spread this over the top of the cake. Let set. Using a pastry bag fitted with a medium star tip, pipe 8 rosettes of the remaining filling around the rim of the cake and decorate each one with a candied coffee bean.

ANNIE'S FAT-FREE FRUIT LOAVES

SERVES 20–24

3 cups golden raisins (sultanas)
1¼ cups cold tea
1 egg, beaten
1¼ cups light brown sugar
2½ cups self-rising flour
butter, for greasing

Soak the raisins in the tea overnight.

Preheat the oven to 325°F. Grease two loaf pans, about 5×4×2 inches, with butter and line the bottoms with wax or parchment paper.

Beat all the ingredients together until evenly combined. Divide the batter between the pans and bake until risen and firm to the touch, about 1¼ hours (a fine metal skewer inserted into the center will come out clean and hot to the touch).

Let cool in the pans, then unmold on a wire rack. Serve cut in slices, with or without butter.

TUTTI-FRUTTI CAKE

SERVES 8

¾ cup soft tub margarine
¾ cup+2 tbsp sugar
3 eggs
1 ½ cups self-rising flour
pinch of salt
1 tsp baking powder
⅓ cup minced assorted candied fruits, such as cherries
and angelica
butter or vegetable oil, for greasing

FOR THE FILLING

⅔ cup whipping cream, whipped to soft peaks
¼ cup apricot preserves

Preheat the oven to 350°F. Grease two 8-inch layer cake pans with butter or oil and line the bottoms with wax or parchment paper.

Place all the ingredients for the cake except the candied fruits in a large bowl and beat well with a wooden spoon for 1–2 minutes, until the batter has a "soft dropping consistency."

Divide the batter between the two pans and level the surface. Sprinkle the candied fruit evenly over the surface of one of the cakes.

Bake the cakes until risen and just firm to the touch, about 25 minutes. Let cool slightly and then unmold and transfer to wire racks.

Make the filling by combining the cream and apricot preserves and use this to put the cake layers together with the fruit-topped cake layer uppermost.

NOTE: For a more professional finish, bake the cake 10 minutes before sprinkling over the candied fruits.

Center: Tutti-Frutti Cake; top and bottom: Annie's Fat-Free Fruit Loaves

A WORLD OF CAKES

No trip to, say, Vienna or Budapest would be complete without a visit to one of the many coffee shops to taste the wonderful local specialties. Most countries – and many regions within countries – have their own distinctive cakes and pastries, some more famous than others and many you'd love to try over and over again. Mostly they are made with popular or special ingredients grown in that area or characteristic of that region, like German Poppy Seed and Strawberry Cake or Spanish Olive Oil and Sweet Wine Cake. An excellent means of expanding your cake-making repertoire is to take careful note of recipes as you travel and then recreate them at home.

Left: Tropical Cheesecake (page 31); right: Spanish Olive Oil and Sweet Wine Cake (page 31)

COCONUT CAKE

SERVES 8

1 ½ sticks (¾ cup) butter softened, plus more for greasing
¾ cup + 2 tbsp sugar
3 tbsp warm water
3 eggs
1 cup + 2 tbsp self-rising flour
¾ cup dried shredded coconut

Preheat the oven to 350°F. Grease an 8-inch round cake pan with butter and line the bottom and sides with a double thickness of wax or parchment paper.

Cream the butter and sugar until almost white. Beat in the water, 1 tablespoon at a time. Then beat in the eggs one at a time.

Sift in the flour, then add all but 2 tablespoons of the coconut. Fold this into the creamed mixture until evenly combined.

Transfer to the prepared pan and level the surface. Sprinkle with the remaining coconut and bake until risen and golden and just springy to the touch, about 45 minutes.

Let cool slightly in the pan and then unmold on a wire rack.

BANANA LOAF

SERVES 10–12

1 stick (8 tbsp) butter, diced, plus more for greasing
2 cups self-rising flour
½ tsp salt
¾ cup + 2 tbsp sugar
¾ cup golden raisins (sultanas)
½ cup chopped pecans
¾ cup candied cherries, halved
2 eggs, beaten
2 cups mashed ripe bananas

Preheat the oven to 350°F. Grease a loaf pan, about 9×5×3 inch, with butter and line the bottom with wax or parchment paper.

Sift the flour and salt into a large bowl and rub in the butter until the mixture resembles fine crumbs.

Stir in the sugar, raisins, nuts, and cherries until evenly coated with the mixture.

Add the eggs and banana to the mixture and beat well until evenly incorporated.

Transfer to the prepared pan and bake until risen and just firm to the touch, about 1 hour 10 minutes. Let the cake cool in the pan, then unmold on a wire rack.

Dried shredded coconut gives COCONUT CAKE *a moist, crumbly texture that is further enhanced by leaving the cake to mature a couple of days. Wrap it carefully and store in a cool, dry place.*

BANANA LOAF *tastes better if made using well-ripened bananas with blackening skins. The cake also develops in flavor if wrapped and stored a few days before eating.*

TROPICAL CHEESECAKE★

SERVES 10

FOR THE BASE

1 ½ cups ginger-snap or graham-cracker crumbs, firmly packed

6 tbsp butter, melted

FOR THE FILLING

2 eggs, separated

(★see page 2 for advice on eggs)

7 tbsp sugar

½ lb cream cheese

6 tbsp pineapple juice

2 envelopes unflavored gelatin

⅔ cup whipping cream, lightly whipped

1 tsp lemon juice

FOR THE TOPPING

1 tsp arrowroot

¼ cup pineapple juice

½ cup chopped, canned or fresh pineapple

¾ cup chopped fresh mango and/or canned or fresh peach

Line the sides of an 8-inch springform pan with wax or parchment paper.

Make the base: Combine the cookie crumbs and butter and press this mixture in a flat layer on the bottom of the pan. Chill.

Make the filling: Beat the egg yolks and sugar until pale, then beat in the cheese.

Put the pineapple juice into a small pan and sprinkle the gelatin over it. Let soak 5 minutes, then place over very low heat just until the gelatin has dissolved. Remove from the heat and add a little of the cheese mixture. Add the contents of the pan to the rest of the cheese mixture, mix well, and chill until starting to set, about 10 minutes. Beat thoroughly until smooth, then fold in the cream.

Beat the egg whites until quite stiff, then gradually beat in the lemon juice. Add a little egg white to the cheese mixture and fold it in. Then fold the rest in carefully. Pour this filling over the cookie base and chill until set, at least 4 hours, or preferably overnight.

Make the topping: Mix the arrowroot and pineapple juice in a small saucepan and cook, stirring, until thickened. Remove from the heat and stir in the fruit. Let cool slightly, then spread over the top of the cheesecake. Chill until set. Unmold to serve.

SPANISH OLIVE OIL AND SWEET WINE CAKE

SERVES 12–16

1 ¼ cups flour

2 tsp baking powder

½ tsp salt

⅞ cup light olive oil

¾ cup + 2 tbsp sugar

3 eggs

½ cup Moscatel de Valencia or other rich, sweet white dessert wine

butter or vegetable oil, for greasing

fresh grapes or other fruit, for serving (optional)

Preheat the oven to 350°F. Grease an 8-inch square cake pan with butter or oil and line the bottom with wax or parchment paper.

Sift the flour, baking powder, and salt together.

In a large bowl, beat together the olive oil, sugar, and eggs. Then fold in the flour mixture until evenly combined.

Transfer to the prepared pan and bake until risen and golden and just firm to the touch, about 40 minutes.

Spike the top of the cake in several places with a skewer, then spoon on the wine. Let the cake cool completely in the pan.

Serve cut in slices, with fresh grapes or other fruit, if desired.

The use of olive oil speeds the making of cakes such as SPANISH OLIVE OIL AND SWEET WHITE WINE CAKE *as it cuts out the more lengthy process of creaming the butter.*

MOSCATEL DE VALENCIA *is a luscious sweet, full-bodied wine made from muscatel grapes grown in the hillside vineyards of Valencia in eastern Spain.*

The two-tone marbling effect in SUNSHINE MARBLE CAKE is produced by separating eggs and using the yolks in one batter and the whites in the other.

Any soft berry fruits, such as raspberries, loganberries, or blueberries, can be used in place of the blackberries in BLACKBERRY AND APPLE RIPPLE CAKE.

SUNSHINE MARBLE CAKE

SERVES 8–12

1 ½ sticks (¾ cup) butter, softened, plus more for greasing
¾ cup + 2 tbsp sugar, plus more for dusting
1 ¼ cups flour, plus more for dusting
3 tbsp orange juice
finely grated zest from 1 large washed orange
3 eggs, separated
2 ¼ tsp baking powder
⅓ cup ground almonds
1 ½ tbsp hot water
pinch of salt

Preheat the oven to 350°F. Grease an 8¾-inch (1½-quart capacity) kugelhopf mold with butter. Sprinkle liberally with sugar and flour and shake well to coat the inside of the mold evenly.

Cream the butter and sugar until almost white, then divide the mixture into two equal portions.

To one portion, add the orange juice, a little at a time. Then add the orange zest and egg yolks and beat thoroughly.

Sift half the flour with 1½ teaspoons of baking powder and fold this into the orange mixture together with half the ground almonds.

To the other portion of butter mixture, add the hot water and beat well.

Sift the remaining flour, baking powder, and ground almonds together.

Beat the egg whites with a pinch of salt until stiff. Then fold alternate spoonfuls of them and the sifted flour mixture into the hot water and butter mixture.

Place alternate spoonfuls of the orange batter and this white batter in the prepared mold.

Bake until risen and just firm to the touch, about 40 minutes. Let the cake cool in the mold until just cool enough to handle, then immediately unmold on a wire rack.

BLACKBERRY AND APPLE RIPPLE CAKE

SERVES 8–10

1 ½ sticks (¾ cup) butter, softened, plus more for greasing
1 cup sugar
3 eggs
1 ½ cups self-rising flour
nearly 2 cups blackberries
2 apples, peeled, cored, and grated

Preheat the oven to 350°F. Line the bottom of a 9-inch round cake pan with wax or parchment paper and grease it with butter.

Reserve 2 tablespoons sugar. Cream the butter with the remaining sugar in a large bowl until almost white, then beat in the eggs one at a time until thoroughly incorporated. Fold in the flour.

Spoon about two-thirds of the batter into the prepared pan.

Mix the blackberries, apples, and reserved sugar. Spoon this over the cake batter and then drop spoonfuls of the remaining cake batter over the top in a random pattern.

Bake until risen and golden and just firm to the touch, about 1 hour. Let cool in the pan.

Left: Sunshine Marble Cake; right: Blackberry and Apple Ripple Cake

JEWELED FRUITCAKE

SERVES 16

2 sticks (1 cup) butter, softened, plus more for greasing
1 cup ground almonds
1 ²⁄₃ cups light brown sugar
1 ¼ cups beaten egg (5 extra large eggs)
1 ³⁄₄ cups flour
1 tbsp apple pie spice
3 cups raisins
3 cups golden raisins
1 cup diced mixed candied peel
3 tbsp orange juice
¼ cup sherry wine or dark rum
1 ½ cups candied cherries

FOR DECORATION
4–6 tbsp apricot jam, warmed and strained
6 candied cherries
2 candied pears, quartered
3 candied orange slices, halved
3 candied pineapple slices, halved
2 wedges of candied apple
2 slices of candied kiwi, halved
3 tbsp whole blanched almonds, toasted

Preheat the oven to 300°F. Line the bottom and sides of a 9-inch round cake pan with a double thickness of greased parchment paper, then wrap the outside with a thick layer of brown paper or newspaper.

Place the ground almonds in a frying pan and cook over medium heat, stirring all the time, until evenly toasted. Let cool.

Cream the butter and sugar together in a large bowl until pale and fluffy. Beat in the egg a little at a time until evenly combined.

Fold in the flour, spice, and ground almonds. Then stir in the fruit, orange juice, and sherry or rum and mix thoroughly. Lastly, stir in the cherries.

Transfer the batter to the prepared pan and level the surface.

Bake until just firm to the touch, about 3 hours (a fine metal skewer inserted into the center should come out piping hot and clean). Let cool in the pan.

To decorate: Unmold the cooled cake and brush the surface with some of the warmed apricot preserves. Arrange the candied fruit and toasted nuts attractively over the surface of the cake and brush with the remaining preserves.

CHERRY STREUSEL CAKE

SERVES 12–16

1 stick (8 tbsp) butter, softened, plus more for greasing
1 cup sugar
3 eggs
1 ¼ cups self-rising flour
1 ⅓ cups ground almonds
1 ½ cups candied cherries, quartered
⅓ cup sliced almonds

Preheat the oven to 350°F. Grease a 7-inch round cake pan with butter and line the bottom and sides with a double thickness of wax or parchment paper.

Reserve 6 tablespoons sugar. In a bowl, cream the butter and remaining sugar until almost white. Beat in 2 whole eggs, one at a time. Then separate the third egg and add the yolk. Reserve the white for the topping.

Combine the flour, half the ground almonds, and the cherries and fold this into the creamed mixture. Transfer to the prepared pan and level the surface.

Make the topping by combining the remaining ingredients and scatter this on the top of the cake.

Bake until risen and golden, 1–1¼ hours (a fine metal skewer inserted into the center of the cake should come out clean and feel piping hot to the touch.)

Let the cake cool in the pan, then unmold on a wire rack.

SRI LANKAN FRUITCAKE

SERVES 16

1½ sticks (¾ cup) butter, softened, plus more for greasing
¾ cup raisins, minced
1¼ cups golden raisins (sultanas), minced
⅔ cup diced assorted candied fruits
⅔ cup diced crystallized ginger
⅓ cup diced mixed candied peel
1 cup candied cherries, halved
1 cup minced cashew nuts or blanched almonds
⅔ cup melon and ginger preserves
2 tbsp dark rum
¾ cup+2 tbsp sugar
3 eggs, separated, plus 3 extra yolks
1 tsp finely grated zest from 1 washed lemon
¾ tsp ground cardamon
½ tsp ground cinnamon
½ tsp ground nutmeg
½ tsp ground cloves
1 tbsp pure vanilla extract
⅔ cup semolina flour

Preheat the oven to 300°F. Grease an 8-inch round cake pan with butter and line with a double thickness of parchment paper. Wrap the outside of the pan with newspaper or brown paper.

Combine the fruits, nuts, melon and ginger preserves, and the rum. Cover and let macerate while preparing the cake, or up to 24 hours.

Cream the butter and sugar until almost white then beat in all the egg yolks, one at a time. Then beat in the lemon zest, spices, and vanilla. Stir in the semolina followed by the fruit until evenly mixed.

Beat the egg whites until stiff, then fold them into the fruit mixture.

Transfer to the prepared pan and level the surface. Bake until just firm to the touch, about 2½ hours. Let cool in the pan.

When using CANDIED CHERRIES, *it is always a good idea to rinse and dry them thoroughly to remove excess sugar syrup. Then mix them with some of the flour: This helps prevent them from drifting to the bottom of the cake during baking.*

YVONNE'S YOGURT CAKE

SERVES 8

½ cup vegetable oil or melted butter, softened, plus
more for greasing
½ cup plain yogurt
1 cup sugar
2 eggs
1¼ cups flour
1½ tsp baking powder
finely grated zest of 1 washed lemon or 1 tbsp orange
blossom water
strawberry or raspberry preserves or fresh berries, for
serving (optional)

Preheat the oven to 350°F. Grease the bottom of an 8¾-inch round cake pan with oil or butter and line the bottom with wax or parchment paper.

Mix the yogurt and sugar in a large bowl until smooth, then beat in the oil or melted butter and the eggs until well combined.

Sift the flour and baking powder together and beat them into the mixture. Then stir in the lemon zest or orange blossom water.

Transfer the batter to the prepared pan and bake until risen and just firm to the touch, about 45 minutes. Let cool in the pan, then transfer to a wire rack.

Serve with preserves or fresh berries, if using, to accompany morning coffee.

Clockwise from the top: Poppy Seed and Strawberry Cake, Cherry Streusel Cake (page 35), and Yvonne's Yogurt Cake

POPPY SEED AND STRAWBERRY CAKE

SERVES 12

⅔ cup poppy seeds
1 cup milk
2 sticks (1 cup) butter, softened, plus more for greasing
1⅔ cups light brown sugar
3 eggs, separated
1⅔ cups whole wheat flour
1½ tsp baking powder
pinch of salt
6 tbsp strawberry preserves, warmed

Place the poppy seeds and milk in a saucepan and bring to a boil. Then remove from the heat and let infuse at least 20 minutes (leaving it for longer won't matter).

Preheat the oven to 350°F. Grease an 8¾-inch round cake pan with butter and line the bottom and sides with a double thickness of wax or parchment paper.

Cream the butter and sugar together in a large bowl until light and fluffy, then beat in the egg yolks one at a time.

Mix the flour and baking powder together and fold alternate large spoonfuls of this and the poppy seed mixture into the creamed mixture.

Beat the egg whites with a pinch of salt until stiff and then fold into the batter.

Transfer to the pan and level the surface. Bake until risen and just springy to the touch, 1–1¼ hours. Cool in the pan, then unmold on a wire rack.

Brush the top of the cake with the warmed preserves and let cool.

YVONNE'S YOGURT CAKE *is a French plain cake to be eaten for breakfast or with morning coffee, on its own or with preserves.*

Before making POPPY SEED AND STRAWBERRY CAKE, *it is essential to soak the poppy seeds in the milk to soften them; this makes the cake more moist. Any fruit preserves can be used to top the cake, and then it can be served with the corresponding fresh fruit.*

CHOCOLATE SPONGE CAKE

SERVES 8

1 stick (8 tbsp) butter, softened, plus more for greasing
1 cup self-rising flour
1 tsp baking powder
⅓ cup unsweetened cocoa powder
3 tbsp boiling water
3 tbsp light corn syrup
½ cup + 2 tbsp granulated sugar
3 eggs, beaten
⅔ cup whipping cream, whipped to soft peaks
confectioners' sugar, for dusting

When adding the eggs to the CHOCOLATE SPONGE CAKE *mixture, stir in a spoonful of the flour, if necessary, to prevent curdling.*

Traditional to Viennese pastry-making GRIESTORTE *is commonly made using semolina flour and probably owes its origins to Turkish influence.*

Preheat the oven to 350°F. Grease an 8¾-inch round cake pan with butter, then line the bottom with wax or parchment paper.

Sift the flour and baking powder into a bowl. In another bowl mix the cocoa, water, and corn syrup until smooth. In a large bowl, cream the butter and sugar until almost white. Beat in the eggs a little at a time. Fold in the flour, then the cocoa mixture.

Transfer the batter to the pan and bake until risen and just firm to the touch, about 35 minutes.

Let cool slightly, then unmold on a rack. Leave the pan over the cake until cold. To serve, split the cake into 2 equal layers and fill with whipped cream. Dust the top with confectioners' sugar.

RED BERRY GRIESTORTE

SERVES 8

1 cup + 2 tbsp granulated sugar, plus more for dusting
6 eggs, separated
finely grated zest and juice of 1 washed lemon
⅔ cup rice flour or semolina flour
⅓ cup ground almonds
pinch of salt
about 1½ cups red berries
⅔ cup whipping cream, whipped to soft peaks
butter, for greasing
confectioners' sugar, for dusting

Preheat the oven to 350°F. Grease two 8-inch layer cake pans with butter and line the bottom with wax or parchment paper. Sprinkle the sides of the pans with sugar to coat them evenly. Shake out any excess.

Beat the egg yolks, ¾ cup sugar, and the lemon juice in a large bowl until thick and pale. Then stir in the lemon zest, rice or semolina flour, and the ground almonds until smooth.

Beat the egg whites with a pinch of salt until stiff, then beat in the remaining sugar a little at a time.

Fold the egg yolk mixture into the egg whites. Divide the batter between the prepared pans.

Bake until risen and just firm to the touch, about 30 minutes. Let cool slightly in the pans, then unmold on wire racks.

Fold the red berries into the whipped cream and use this to sandwich the cake layers together. Dust the top with confectioners' sugar.

APPLESAUCE CAKE

SERVES 10–12

1 lb cooking apples, peeled, cored, and chopped
1 cup + 2 tbsp granulated sugar, plus more for dusting
3 tbsp chopped candied cherries
⅓ cup toasted sliced almonds
3 tbsp dried currants
1 tbsp chopped candied angelica
1 stick (8 tbsp) butter, softened, plus more for greasing
1⅔ cups flour, plus more for dusting
1 egg
1 tsp baking soda
pinch of salt
1 cup confectioners' sugar, sifted
1 tbsp apple juice
candied fruits, for decoration (optional)

Place the apples in a pan with 4 tablespoons of the granulated sugar and cook gently to a purée, about 10 minutes. Continue cooking over medium heat, stirring all the time, until really thick, about 5 minutes longer. Let cool completely, then stir in the cherries, almonds, currants, and angelica.

Preheat the oven to 350°F. Grease a 9½-inch ring mold with butter, then dust the inside with a little sugar and flour. Shake out any excess.

Cream the butter and half the remaining granulated sugar until almost white, then beat in the remaining granulated sugar and egg.

Sift the flour, baking soda, and salt together and fold this into the creamed mixture. Stir in the applesauce and transfer the batter to the mold.

Bake until risen and firm to the touch, about 35 minutes. Let cool slightly in the mold, then unmold on a wire rack and let cool completely.

Mix the confectioners' sugar with the apple juice to give a thick, smooth icing and drizzle it over the cooled cake. Decorate with extra candied fruits, if using, and let set.

DATE, PEAR, AND WALNUT CAKE

SERVES 8–10

⅔ cup pitted dates
⅓ cup date syrup or malt extract
½ cup vegetable oil
½ cup plain yogurt or buttermilk
2 eggs
1 cup whole wheat flour
½ tsp baking soda
1 tsp ground cinnamon
½ tsp apple pie spice
¾ cup walnut pieces
2 ripe pears
¼ cup apricot jam, warmed and strained
butter or vegetable oil, for greasing

Place the dates in a small saucepan with ⅔ water and cook until all the water has evaporated, to produce a soft date purée. Let cool.

Preheat the oven to 350°F and grease a 9-inch springform pan with butter or oil.

Place the date syrup or malt extract in a large bowl with the oil, yogurt or buttermilk, and the eggs and beat until smooth. Then beat in the date purée.

Mix the flour, baking soda, and spices together and fold them into the date mixture with the walnuts. Transfer to the prepared pan.

Peel, quarter, and core the pears. Then cut each quarter into thin slices without cutting completely through the top of each piece. Fan out the slices of each pear quarter and place them attractively on top of the cake batter.

Bake until the cake is risen and just firm to the touch, 45–50 minutes.

Let cool in the pan, then transfer to a wire rack. Brush with the warmed and strained apricot jam and let cool.

ELABORATE CAKES AND TORTES

The elegant confections that grace bakery windows have helped generate the myth that such cakes are only to be bought and hardly ever to be made. However, that really need not be the case. There is no doubt that elaborate cakes are fairly time-consuming to put together, but the process can often be spread over a couple of days – the cake layers baked on one day and the assembly and decoration completed the next.

All the recipes in this chapter are relatively approachable and very tasty, using the full flavors of citrus fruits, berries, chocolate, nuts, and liqueurs with the richness of butter-creams or whipped cream. Final presentation is all-important and there is no substitute for practice to achieve the right finish.

Pavlova Palette (page 42)

CARROT AND PASSION FRUIT LAYER CAKE

SERVES 12–16

1 ¼ cups raisins
1 ¼ cups sunflower oil, plus more for greasing
1 ⅔ cups flour
2 tsp baking powder
1 tsp baking soda
1 tsp salt
1 tsp ground cinnamon
4 eggs
2 tsp pure vanilla extract
1 cup + 2 tbsp granulated sugar
1 ¼ cups light brown sugar
2 cups chopped walnuts
1 lb carrots, finely grated and excess moisture squeezed out

FOR THE PASSION FRUIT ICING

4 passion fruit, halved
2 cups confectioners' sugar, sifted
1 tsp lemon juice
2 sticks (1 cup) butter, softened
½ cup cream cheese

A classic of Antipodean cooking that has become an international favorite, the PAVLOVA *meringue cake was devised in honor of the great Russian prima ballerina when she toured Australia early this century.*

Put the raisins in a small saucepan with just enough water to cover and simmer until they are well plumped up, about 10 minutes. Let cool completely and then drain thoroughly.

Preheat the oven to 350°F. Grease three 9-inch round cake pans with oil and line the bottoms with wax or parchment paper.

Sift the flour, baking powder, soda, salt, and cinnamon together. Beat the eggs, vanilla, sugars, and oil in a bowl until thick. Fold in the flour mixture, followed by the walnuts, raisins, and carrot.

Transfer the batter to the prepared pans and bake until risen and just firm to the touch, about 25 minutes. Let the cakes cool in the pans, then carefully unmold them on wire racks.

Make the passion fruit icing: Place the pulp from the passion fruit in a saucepan with 2 tablespoons of the sugar, the lemon juice, and 2 tablespoons water. Simmer until the pulp loosens from the seeds, 2–3 minutes. Pass the contents of the pan through a fine strainer and let cool.

Beat the butter until smooth, then beat in the remaining sugar, a little at a time. Beat in the cream cheese and stir in the passion fruit purée.

Use a little of this mixture to sandwich the cake layers together, then use the rest to cover the top and sides of the cake.

PAVLOVA PALETTE

SERVES 12–16

4 egg whites (about ¾ cup)
pinch of salt
1 cup + 2 tbsp superfine sugar
2 tsp cornstarch
1 tsp vinegar
1 tsp pure vanilla extract
2 ½ cups whipping cream, whipped into soft peaks
selection of prepared fruits in season
confectioners' sugar, for dusting

Preheat the oven to 300°F.

Draw a circle on a piece of 10-inch nonstick silicone paper and set it on a baking sheet.

Beat the egg whites with a pinch of salt until stiff, then beat in the superfine sugar, 1 tablespoonful at a time, adding the cornstarch with the last spoonful. Quickly beat in the vinegar and vanilla.

Transfer the mixture to the paper and spread it evenly, making a slight dip in the center. Bake 1 hour, then switch off the oven and leave the meringue in the oven to cool completely.

Spread the whipped cream over the top of the cold pavlova, then cover with an abstract arrangement of fruits. Dust with confectioners' sugar.

SAFFRON LAYER CAKE

SERVES 10–12

½ tsp saffron threads
4 eggs
¾ cup + 2 tbsp sugar
1 cup cake flour
1 tbsp baking powder
1 tsp ground cardamon
⅓ cup sunflower seeds
⅓ cup minced pistachio nuts
butter, for greasing
FOR THE FROSTING AND DECORATION
1 ½ sticks (¾ cup) unsalted butter, softened
¾ cup cream cheese
3 cups confectioners' sugar, sifted
2 tbsp lemon juice
1–2 tbsp milk

Mix the saffron with 2 tablespoons of boiling water in a bowl and let infuse 10 minutes.

Preheat the oven to 350°F. Grease three 8-inch layer cake pans with butter and line the bottoms with wax or parchment paper.

Beat the eggs, saffron (with liquid), and sugar in a large bowl set over simmering water until thick and mousse-like and the beaters leave a trail. Sift in the flour, baking powder, and cardamon and fold into the mixture. Fold in the seeds and most of the nuts.

Transfer the batter to the prepared pans and bake until risen and just firm to the touch, about 20 minutes. Let cool on wire racks.

Make the frosting: Beat the butter and cheese until smooth. Beat in the sugar and juice, followed by enough milk to give a spreadable consistency.

Use about one-third to sandwich the cake layers together. Put about one-quarter of the remainder in a pastry bag fitted with a star tip. Spread the rest over the top and sides, then pipe whirls around the edge and sprinkle with the reserved pistachios.

CHESTNUT CREAM CAKE

SERVES 10–12

1 lb peeled cooked chestnuts
4 tbsp butter, melted, plus more for greasing
½ cup cake flour
pinch of salt
4 eggs
few drops of pure vanilla extract
¾ cup + 2 tbsp sugar
FOR THE CHESTNUT CREAM
½ cup confectioners' sugar, sifted
¼ cup milk
1 ¼ cups whipping cream, whipped to soft peaks
maraschino cherries (preferably with stems), for decoration

Preheat the oven to 375°F. Grease three 8-inch layer cake pans with butter, then line the bottoms with wax or parchment paper. Push the chestnuts through a fine strainer. Sift the flour and salt.

Beat the eggs, vanilla, and sugar together in a large bowl set over a saucepan of simmering water, until the mixture is thick and mousse-like and the beaters leave a trail. Remove from the heat.

Put half of the chestnut purée in a bowl and stir a quarter of the egg mixture into it until smooth. Then fold this into the rest of the egg mixture. Fold in the sifted flour, followed by the butter.

Divide among the pans and bake until risen and just firm to the touch, about 15 minutes. Let cool in the pans, then transfer to wire racks.

Make the chestnut cream: Mix the remaining chestnut purée with the sugar and milk. Alternatively, work them together in a food processor until smooth. Fold the mixture into the cream and flavor to taste with a little of the syrup from the cherries.

Use a little of the cream to put the cake layers together, then spread the rest over the top and sides of the cake. Decorate with maraschino cherries.

One of the most valued and expensive of spices, SAFFRON is made from the dried stigma of a variety of crocus. It is highly favored in the cooking of both sweet and savory dishes for its rich color and subtle flavor.

ORANGE FLORENTINE CAKE

Despite their Italian name, the familiar chocolate-backed caramel cookies studded with nuts and crystallized fruit, known as FLORENTINES, are actually a specialty of Austrian and German pastry shops.

SERVES 12

½ cup cake flour, plus more for dusting
1 ¼ cups confectioners' sugar, sifted
3 eggs, plus 3 egg yolks
1 tbsp finely grated zest from 1 washed orange
2 tbsp orange liqueur
7 tbsp potato flour or cornstarch
pinch of salt
butter, for greasing
granulated sugar, for dusting
FOR THE FROSTING
3 ½ tbsp custard powder or cornstarch
1 ¼ cups milk
2 egg yolks
1 ¼ cups confectioners' sugar
2 sticks (1 cup) unsalted butter, softened
3 tbsp orange juice
FOR THE FLORENTINE TOPPING
¾ cup granulated sugar
½ cup sliced almonds, toasted

Preheat the oven to 325°F. Grease an 8¾-inch springform cake pan with butter, then line the bottom with wax or parchment paper. Dust the sides with a little sugar and flour, then shake out any excess.

In a large bowl set over a pan of simmering water, beat the confectioners' sugar with all the eggs and extra yolks, the orange zest, and the liqueur until thick and foamy. Sift together the flour, potato flour, and salt and fold into the beaten mixture.

Transfer to the prepared pan and bake until risen and just firm to the touch, about 25 minutes. Let cool slightly in the pan, then transfer to a wire rack. Let cool completely.

Make the frosting: Mix the custard powder or cornstarch with a little of the milk and the egg yolks to give a smooth paste.

Heat the remaining milk with a sprinkling of the sugar until just below boiling point. Then pour this over the custard and mix until smooth. Return this mixture to the saucepan and cook, stirring, until thickened. Transfer to a bowl, cover, and let cool. When cold, beat until smooth.

Beat the butter and remaining sugar until smooth. Then beat in the custard, a little at a time, until smooth. Then beat in the orange juice in the same way.

Make the Florentine topping: Cut an 8-inch round of foil and grease it generously with butter. Place the sugar in a saucepan over medium heat and cook to a light caramel color. Stir in the nuts and immediately pour this caramel on the foil, spreading it quickly with a buttered knife. Let cool slightly, then mark it into 8 wedges using a buttered sharp knife. Let cool completely, then break it into wedges as marked.

Split the cake into 3 equal layers and use a generous third of the frosting to sandwich the layers together. Use most of the rest to cover the top and sides of the cake. Using a pastry bag fitted with a star tip, pipe 8 rosettes of the remaining frosting at regular intervals around the edge of the top of the cake. Then set the Florentine wedges on top of the cake, each resting at a similar angle on the rosettes. Then pipe one more rosette in the center, and chill until required.

NOTE: It is best to make this cake the day before it is needed. The Florentine topping can also be made the day before and stored in buttered foil.

Left: Lemon Syrup Layer Cake (page 50); center: Orange Florentine Cake

DOUBLE TRUFFLE TORTE★

SERVES 16–20

FOR THE CAKE LAYERS

½ cup cake flour, plus more for dusting
½ cup + 2 tbsp sugar, plus more for dusting
2 tbsp cornstarch
¼ cup unsweetened cocoa powder, plus more for dusting
4 eggs
butter, for greasing

FOR THE DARK TRUFFLE LAYER

3 oz semisweet chocolate
2 tbsp milk
1 stick (8 tbsp) unsalted butter
½ cup + 2 tbsp sugar
¾ cup unsweetened cocoa powder, sifted
3 egg yolks
(★see page 2 for advice on eggs)
1 cup crème fraîche or whipping cream

FOR THE WHITE TRUFFLE LAYER

3 oz white chocolate
1 stick (8 tbsp) unsalted butter
½ cup + 2 tbsp sugar
¾ cup ground almonds
3 egg yolks
1 cup crème fraîche or whipping cream

Preheat the oven to 375°F. Butter three 8-inch layer cake pans and line the bottoms with wax or parchment paper. Dust the sides with a mixture of equal parts flour and sugar, then shake out any excess. Sift the flour, cornstarch, and cocoa together.

Place the eggs and sugar in a large bowl set over a saucepan of simmering water and beat until thick and foamy (the beaters should leave a thick trail in the mixture).

Fold in the flour mixture and divide among the pans. Bake until just firm to the touch, 10–15 minutes. Unmold and let cool on wire racks.

Line the bottom and sides of an 8-inch spring-form cake pan with a 3½-inch collar of nonstick silicone paper.

Make the dark truffle layer: Melt the chocolate with the milk and stir until smooth. Let cool.

Beat the butter and sugar together in a bowl until light and fluffy, then beat in the chocolate mixture, cocoa, egg yolks, and crème fraîche or cream.

Place one cake layer in the prepared pan and spread the dark truffle mixture on top. Set a second cake layer on top and press lightly. Chill.

Make the white truffle layer: Melt the chocolate and stir until smooth. Let cool.

Beat the butter and sugar together in a bowl until light and fluffy, then beat in the chocolate, ground almonds, egg yolks, and crème fraîche or cream.

Spread the white truffle mixture on top of the cake layer and cover with the last layer. Press down lightly and chill 24 hours.

Unmold and dust with cocoa powder before serving, cut in very thin wedges.

The candies known as chocolate TRUFFLES, due to their physical similarity to the equally delicious little black truffle fungus, are traditionally given as Christmas gifts in France. They are classically flavored with rum or praline, but brandy, Scotch, champagne, and vanilla truffles are also common.

PEAR GALETTE

SERVES 8

FOR THE PASTRY
1 cup finely ground, toasted almonds
6 tbsp butter
3 tbsp sugar
¾ cup+2 tbsp flour
pinch of salt

FOR THE FILLING
2 lb pears, peeled, cored, and chopped
1 tbsp apricot preserves
finely grated zest of ½ washed lemon
1 tbsp diced mixed candied peel
2 tbsp dried currants
2 tbsp golden raisins (sultanas)

FOR THE DECORATION
about ½ cup whipped cream
8 toasted skinned hazelnuts
confectioners' sugar, for dusting

Make the pastry: Work all the ingredients in a food processor until evenly combined. Chill 20 minutes.

Cut the dough in half and roll out each piece to form a 9-inch round on a circle of nonstick silicone paper. Chill on baking sheets for 20 minutes.

Preheat the oven to 375°F and bake the pastry rounds until golden, about 20 minutes. Cut one into 8 even wedges. Let cool completely.

Make the filling: Place the ingredients in a pan and cook over medium heat, stirring occasionally, until the pears are soft and all the juice has evaporated, about 15 minutes. Let cool.

Just before serving, place the pastry round on a plate and spread with filling. Set the wedges on top and dust with confectioners' sugar. Decorate with piped "shells" of cream and top with hazelnuts.

Left to right: Marzipan Petal Cake (page 51), Pear Galette, and Coconut Cheesecake with Strawberry Coulis (page 50)

COFFEE-WALNUT GÂTEAU

SERVES 12

2 tbsp espresso coffee granules dissolved in 2 tbsp boiling water
6 eggs
1 cup+2 tbsp sugar
1⅓ cups finely ground walnuts
1½ cups cake flour
1 tsp baking powder
2 tbsp walnut oil
¼ cup apricot preserves
12 candied coffee beans
butter, for greasing

FOR THE COFFEE BUTTERCREAM
1 tbsp espresso coffee granules
½ cup milk
4 egg yolks
½ cup+2 tbsp sugar
2 sticks+1 tbsp (17 tbsp) unsalted butter, diced

Preheat the oven to 350°F. Butter two 8-inch round cake pans and line with wax or parchment paper.

Mix a batter as on page 47, adding coffee to the eggs and sugar, and walnuts to the sifted flour. Fold in the walnut oil. Divide between the pans and bake 25 minutes. Cool in the pans, then unmold on racks.

Make the buttercream: In a small pan over very low heat, dissolve the coffee in the milk. Beat the egg yolks and sugar in a bowl, then pour on the milk and stir well. Return to the pan and cook gently until thick enough to coat the back of a spoon. Strain, cover, and cool. Beat in butter, a little at a time, to make a thick buttercream.

Split each cake into 2 layers and sandwich the pairs together with a little buttercream. Put the two cakes together with preserves. Reserving 6 tablespoons, use the rest of the buttercream to cover the top and sides. Pipe 12 rosettes of buttercream around the top. Top each with a coffee bean.

The stirred custard for the coffee buttercream used in the COFFEE WALNUT GATEAU can also be thickened by cooking it in the microwave oven for 3 minutes, whisking after each minute.

In French cooking,
a COULIS is a thin
purée or sauce of
raw or cooked
vegetables or fruit.
Fruit coulis are
popular
accompaniments to
all sorts of desserts,
especially frozen
ones.

COCONUT CHEESECAKE WITH STRAWBERRY COULIS

SERVES 8–12

FOR THE BASE
7 tbsp butter, softened
¼ cup sugar
½ cup flour, sifted
1 tsp baking powder
1 extra large egg, beaten
½ cup dried shredded coconut

FOR THE FILLING
½ lb cream cheese
3 eggs, separated
½ cup + 2 tbsp sugar
3 tbsp flour
⅔ cup canned coconut milk
1 tbsp lemon juice

FOR THE STRAWBERRY COULIS
1 pint ripe strawberries, hulled
½ cup confectioners' sugar
squeeze of lemon juice

FOR DECORATION
⅔ cup whipping cream, whipped to soft peaks
2 fresh strawberries, quartered
1 tbsp shredded coconut, toasted

Make the base: Beat the ingredients together in a bowl until creamy. Using a spatula, spread a thin layer of the mixture on the sides of a 9-inch nonstick springform cake pan. Spread the rest on the bottom. Chill at least 20 minutes. Preheat the oven to 325°F.

Make the filling: Beat the cream cheese, egg yolks, and half the sugar in a bowl until smooth, then beat in the flour and coconut milk.

Beat the egg whites until fairly stiff, then beat in the lemon juice, a little at a time. Beat in the remaining sugar a spoonful at a time. Fold this into the cheese mixture and transfer to the prepared pan.

Bake until lightly golden, about 35 minutes.

Switch off the oven and let the cheesecake cool in it for 10 minutes before removing. Let cool completely.

Make the strawberry coulis: Put the strawberries in a blender or food processor and purée until smooth. Sweeten and add lemon juice to taste. Pass through a fine strainer to remove seeds, if desired.

Unmold the cheesecake and decorate with rosettes of whipped cream, strawberry quarters, and a little toasted coconut. Serve with the strawberry coulis.

LEMON LAYER SYRUP CAKE

SERVES 10–12

1 ¼ cups sugar, plus more for dusting
¾ cup flour, plus more for dusting
2 washed lemons
4 eggs
2 tbsp lukewarm water
7 tbsp cornstarch or potato flour
1 tsp baking powder
butter, for greasing

FOR THE FILLINGS AND TOPPINGS
2 ½ cups whipping cream
3 tbsp confectioners' sugar
½ cup minced pistachio nuts
8 fresh strawberries, for decoration

Preheat the oven to 375°F. Butter a 9-inch round cake pan and line the bottom with wax or parchment paaper. Dust the sides of the pan with a little sugar and flour. Shake out any excess.

Finely grate the zest of one lemon and pare the zest of the other. Extract the juice from them both.

In a large bowl set over a saucepan of simmering water, beat the eggs with the lukewarm water, ¾ cup of the sugar, and the grated lemon zest until thick and mousse-like (the beaters should leave a thick trail in the mixture). Remove from the heat.

Sift the flour, cornstarch, and baking powder together and carefully fold into the mixture. Transfer to the prepared pan and bake until risen and just firm to the touch, about 25 minutes.

Let cool in the pan, then unmold on a wire rack. When cold, split into 3 layers.

Place the pared lemon zest and all the lemon juice in a pan with the remaining sugar and 1¼ cups of water. Heat gently until the sugar dissolves, then boil until the liquid is reduced to about ¾ cup. Strain this syrup and let it cool. Brush the syrup over one of the cut surfaces of each cake layer.

Make the filling: Whip the cream with the sugar to stiff peaks. Use a generous third of this to sandwich the cake layers back together.

Cover the top and sides of the cake with most of the remaining cream. Press the pistachios into the sides of the cake. Using a pastry bag fitted with a star tip and filled with the remaining cream, pipe a ring of shells around the rim of the cake.

Chill until required, then decorate with fruit.

MARZIPAN PETAL CAKE★

SERVES 10

2 tbsp butter, melted, plus more for greasing
½ cup+2 tbsp sugar, plus more for dusting
½ cup cake flour, plus more for dusting
4 eggs
finely grated zest from ½ washed lemon
3½ tbsp cornstarch
½ tsp baking powder
¾ cup ground almonds
FOR THE FILLING AND TOPPING
1 lb 2 oz white marzipan
about 5 tbsp egg whites (about 2 eggs)
(★see page 2 for advice on eggs)
about ½ cup raspberry preserves
⅔ cup sliced almonds, lightly toasted

Preheat the oven to 350°F. Grease an 8½-inch springform cake pan with butter, then line the bottom with wax or parchment paper. Coat the sides with a little sugar and flour and shake out any excess.

In a large bowl set over simmering water, beat the eggs, sugar, and lemon zest until thick and mousse-like. Remove from the heat and continue beating until cool.

Sift the flour, cornstarch, baking powder, and ground almonds together and fold them into the mixture, followed by the melted butter.

Transfer the batter to the prepared pan and bake until risen and golden and just firm to the touch, about 25 minutes. Let cool in the pan, then unmold on a wire rack. (This cake is best made the day before.)

Make the filling: Place half the marzipan and 3 tablespoons of the egg white in a food processor and work until smooth and soft enough to spread.

Split the cake into 2 layers and then sandwich the layers together with about 6 tablespoons of the preserves. Set on a baking sheet.

Use the marzipan-egg white mixture to cover the top and sides of the cake, then press the toasted almonds all over the sides to cover them completely.

Preheat the oven to its highest setting.

Put the rest of the marzipan in the food processor with 5 tablespoons of egg white and work until smooth enough to pipe. Using a pastry bag fitted with a small star tip and starting in the center of the cake, pipe about 10 loops of the marzipan mixture to the outside edge to create the impression of the petals of a flower. Pipe a rosette in the center.

Bake the cake until golden brown, about 10 minutes. Then remove from the oven and let cool. Fill each "petal" with about ½ teaspoon of preserves and let it cool completely.

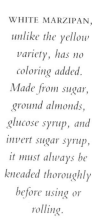

WHITE MARZIPAN, *unlike the yellow variety, has no coloring added. Made from sugar, ground almonds, glucose syrup, and invert sugar syrup, it must always be kneaded thoroughly before using or rolling.*

The curd cheese
RICOTTA *is popular*
in all sorts of
Italian dishes. Its
delicious sweet
flavor makes it a
popular dessert on
its own with fruit
or honey. Use
strained cottage
cheese if you can't
find ricotta.

The bittersweet
Italian liqueur
STREGA *is brewed*
using over 70 herbs.

ITALIAN HAZELNUT CAKE

SERVES 10–12

¾ cup skinned hazelnuts
1 stick (8 tbsp) butter, softened plus more for greasing
½ cup + 2 tbsp sugar
4 eggs, separated
½ cup ricotta cheese
2 tsp finely grated zest from 1 washed lemon
3 tbsp flour, sifted
pinch of salt

FOR DECORATION
4 oz semisweet chocolate, melted
6 tbsp apricot preserves, warmed
1¼ cups whipping cream, whipped to soft peaks
confectioners' sugar, for dusting

Preheat the oven to 400°F and toast the nuts 15–20 minutes. Let cool, then grind them to a fine powder.

Reduce the oven setting to 375°F. Grease a 10-inch layer cake pan or tart pan with butter and line the bottom with wax or parchment paper.

Cream the butter with two-thirds of the sugar in a large bowl until almost white, then beat in the egg yolks, cheese, and lemon zest. Fold the hazelnuts and flour into the creamed mixture.

Beat the egg whites with a pinch of salt until standing in soft peaks. Beat in the remaining sugar and then fold this into the creamed mixture.

Transfer the batter to the prepared pan and bake about 25 minutes. Let cool in the pan, then transfer to a wire rack.

To decorate: Spread the chocolate thinly on a marble slab or smooth plastic work surface and let it set. Using a large knife held at a 45-degree angle to the surface of the chocolate and with the blade facing away from you, scrape curls from the chocolate and set these on a tray in the refrigerator to harden.

Spread the surface of the cake with preserves, then top with whipped cream and the chocolate curls. Finally, dust with confectioners' sugar.

CLEMENTINE-STREGA CAKE

SERVES 16

FOR THE FRUIT LAYER
¾ lb candied whole clementines (mandarins)
½ cup + 2 tbsp sugar
⅔ cup Strega liqueur
FOR THE CAKE LAYERS
½ cup soft tub margarine or 1 stick (8 tbsp) softened butter, plus more for greasing
½ cup + 2 tbsp sugar
2 eggs
¾ cup self-rising flour
⅓ cup unsweetened cocoa powder, sifted
FOR THE CHOCOLATE MIXTURE
1½ cups chocolate-hazelnut fudge sauce
10 oz semisweet chocolate, melted

First make the fruit layer: Place the clementines in a saucepan and just cover with water. Bring to a fast boil, then remove from the heat and let cool in the liquid. Drain, reserving ½ cup of cooking liquid.

Mince the fruit or work in a food processor, then mix it with the reserved liquid and the sugar in a saucepan. Cook over medium heat, stirring occasionally, until thick and syrupy (rather like marmalade), 10–15 minutes. Remove from the heat and stir in two-thirds of the Strega. Let cool completely.

Preheat the oven to 375°F. Grease two loaf pans, measuring about 9×5×3 inches, with butter and line the bottoms with wax or parchment paper.

Make the cake layers: Cream the margarine or butter and sugar together until almost white, then beat in the eggs one at a time. Divide the mixture in ½ cup flour into one portion and the remaining flour and cocoa powder into the other.

Spread one batter in each pan, making a dip in the center of each. Bake until risen and just firm to the touch, about 20 minutes. Let cool on wire racks, then trim the crusts to give two layers each about ¾-inch thick.

Line one of the loaf pans with plastic wrap. Prepare the chocolate mixture by mixing four-fifths of each of the ingredients together. Pour half of this mixture into the bottom of the pan and freeze until solid.

Set one cake layer on top of the frozen chocolate layer and moisten with half of the remaining Strega. Top with the fruit mixture, followed by the other cake layer, and moisten with the last of the Strega. Spread the remaining chocolate mixture on top and freeze until solid, about 1 hour.

Prepare the remaining chocolate mixture ingredients. Unmold the cake and spread the sides with the mixture.

Chill until set, then cut the cake into thin slices for serving.

Top: Italian Hazelnut Cake; bottom: Clementine-Strega Cake

HOLIDAY AND PARTY CAKES

*T*he amazing increase in party cakes now on display in our supermarkets and bakeries shows how popular they have become. Most children – or adults, for that matter – would be pleased to be presented with a special cake on a birthday, anniversary, or other important occasion. Such cakes don't have to be elaborate, but they should be based on fantasy, fun, or fact and reflect some aspect of the season, occasion, or the personality of the recipient.

The cakes in this chapter are also not just limited in their use to unique celebrations, or holidays. They can also be used for a variety of occasions. For instance, the Croquembouche Cooler – as well as making a wonderful anniversary cake – is ideal for giving a really spectacular end to any dinner party.

Pumpkin Cake (page 57)

English SIMNEL
CAKE *seems to have
an ancient history
as a way of
celebrating spring.
At one time it was
a Mothering
Sunday treat, but it
later became
associated with
Easter and often has
eleven marzipan
decorations on the
top to symbolize the
loyal disciples.*

EASTER SIMNEL CAKE★

SERVES 16

2 sticks (1 cup) butter, softened, plus more for greasing
1⅔ cups light brown sugar
4 eggs, beaten
finely grated zest of 1 washed orange
1⅔ cups flour
pinch of salt
⅓ cup rice flour
1 tsp baking powder
1½ cups golden raisins (sultanas)
¾ cup dried currants
¾ cup candied cherries, halved
⅓ cup diced mixed candied peel
FOR THE MARZIPAN
2⅔ cups ground almonds
1 cup+2 tbsp sugar
¼ cup beaten egg
(★see page 2 for advice on eggs)
1 tbsp orange juice

Preheat the oven to 325°F. Grease an 8-inch round cake pan with butter, then line it with a double thickness of wax or parchment paper.

Cream the butter and sugar until pale and fluffy. Beat in the eggs and orange zest a little at a time, adding a spoonful of flour to prevent curdling.

Fold in the remaining flour, the salt, rice flour, and baking powder, then stir in all the fruit.

Make half the quantity of marzipan by combining half of all the ingredients together until smooth. Roll out on a surface lightly sprinkled with confectioners' sugar to make an 8-inch round.

Spoon half the cake batter into the pan and level the surface. Set the marzipan round on top, then spread the remaining cake batter on top.

Bake until risen and just firm to the touch, about 2 hours. Let cool in the pan, then wrap in wax paper and foil and store until required.

To decorate: Make up the rest of the marzipan and roll it out on a surface lightly sprinkled with confectioners' sugar to make another 8-inch round. Trim neatly and press it on top of the cake, then crimp the edges to give a decorative effect.

Use the marzipan trimmings to shape 6 eggs and twist thin rolls of marzipan together to make a nest. Set the eggs in the nest on top of the cake.

SUMMER MERINGUE CAKE

SERVES 12–14

1⅓ cups ground almonds, toasted
⅓ cup+2 tbsp confectioners' sugar, sifted
finely grated zest from ½ washed orange
6 egg whites (9 fl oz)
1 tsp lemon juice
½ cup superfine sugar
FOR THE FILLING AND DECORATION
1 pint raspberry or other fruit sorbet
1 pint best-quality vanilla ice cream
2 cups whipping cream, whipped to soft peaks
*selection of summer fruit, such as raspberries,
blueberries, black currants, and red currants*

Preheat the oven to 325°F. Cut three 9-inch rounds of nonstick silicone paper and set each one on a baking sheet.

Mix the almonds, confectioners' sugar, and orange zest. Beat the egg whites in a bowl until foamy. Gradually beat in the lemon juice drop by drop, and beat until stiff. Then beat in the superfine sugar a spoonful at a time to make a thick, glossy meringue. Fold in the almond mixture and spread the meringue on the paper rounds.

Bake 30 minutes, then let cool. When cold, carefully remove the meringue disks from the paper. Trim the edges if necessary.

Line the bottom and sides of a 9-inch springform pan with nonstick silicone paper. Set one meringue disk in the bottom. Soften the fruit sorbet slightly, beat until smooth, and then spread it on the meringue. Press another meringue disk on top and freeze until firm.

Soften the ice-cream slightly and beat until smooth, then spread it over the meringue. Press the third meringue disk in place, then cover and freeze at least 4 hours or preferably overnight.

When ready to serve: Unmold the cake on a plate. Spread about one-third of the cream over the sides and top of the cake. Using a pastry bag fitted with a star tip, pipe vertical lines of cream up the sides of the cake. Pipe a ring of rosettes around the outside edge of the top. Decorate with the fruit.

PUMPKIN CAKE

SERVES 12–20

3 sticks (1 ½ cups) butter, softened, plus more for greasing
1 ¾ cups sugar
6 eggs, beaten
2 ½ cups self-rising flour
½ cup unsweetened cocoa powder
1 tsp baking powder
FOR THE ICING AND DECORATION
½ cup apricot jam, warmed and strained
1 lb 2 oz fondant icing
orange and green food coloring
confectioners' sugar or cornstarch, for dusting

Preheat the oven to 350°F and butter two 8-inch diameter (1 quart capacity) ovenproof bowls.

Cream the butter and sugar until almost white, then beat in the eggs a little at a time until thoroughly incorporated. Sift the flour, cocoa, and baking powder together and fold into the mixture.

Divide the batter between the bowls and make a slight dip in the center of each. Bake until risen and just firm to the touch, about 1 hour. Cool slightly,

then unmold on a rack and let cool completely. If necessary, trim the top to make them level.

To decorate: sandwich the flat surfaces of the cakes together with a little of the jam, then brush the rest over the sides and top of the whole cake.

Color about five-sixths of the fondant icing with orange coloring and the rest with green.

On a surface lightly sprinkled with confectioners' sugar or cornstarch, roll out the orange icing and use it to cover the cake completely. Press it well to secure, then neaten the base. Using a wooden spoon handle, mark about 12 vertical indentations in the icing to give the impression of the pumpkin surface.

Roll out the green icing thinly and stamp out 5 shapes using a 3-inch star cutter. Press one point of each together to form a stalk and give the look of a leaf, then mark veins with a small knife. Roll tiny pieces of green icing and curl them to make tendrils. Use the remaining icing to make a large stalk. Attach leaves, tendrils, and stalk to the top of the pumpkin using a little water or jam.

CUSTARD BUTTERCREAM

MAKES ABOUT 1½ CUPS

⅔ cup milk
1 ½ tbsp custard powder or cornstarch
1 egg yolk
½ cups+2 tbsp confectioners' sugar, sifted
1 stick (8 tbsp) unsalted butter, softened

Mix 2 tablespoons of the milk with the custard powder and beat in the egg yolk. Put the rest of the milk in a small pan with 2 tablespoons of the sugar and bring to just below a boil.

Pour this over the custard and mix until smooth. Return to the pan and cook, stirring, until thickened. Transfer to a bowl, cover, and let cool.

Beat the butter and remaining sugar until light and fluffy. Then beat this into the custard.

The basic shape of the PUMPKIN CAKE *can be adapted to make other fruit shapes, such as apples or oranges, or into ball shapes. Color the icing as required.* FONDANT ICING *is available at specialty food stores.*

CUSTARD BUTTERCREAM *is useful for filling large cakes like the Kite Cake on page 60. Store it in the refrigerator until needed.*

AUTUMN CHOCOLATE MERINGUE CAKE

SERVES 12–16

1 ½ cups confectioners' sugar
½+2 tbsp unsweetened cocoa powder, plus more for coloring
½ cup hot water
2 ⅔ cups ground hazelnuts, toasted in a frying pan
6 egg whites (9 fl oz)
pinch of salt
½ cup+2 tbsp superfine sugar
butter, for greasing

FOR THE FILLING AND DECORATION

8 oz semisweet chocolate
1 cup light cream
4 oz white marzipan
green and brown food coloring
confectioners' sugar, for dusting

AUTUMN CHOCOLATE MERINGUE CAKE *is a wonderful way of using up spare egg whites. Any other ground nut can replace the hazelnuts, and decorations can be adapted to suit another theme or occasion.*

Preheat the oven to 350°F. Grease two 8½-inch springform cake pans with butter and line the bottoms with nonstick silicone paper.

Sift the confectioners' sugar and cocoa powder into a bowl, then beat in the hot water until the mixture is smooth. Stir in the hazelnuts.

Beat the egg whites with a pinch of salt until stiff, then beat in the superfine sugar a little at a time. Fold about one-quarter of the egg mixture into the chocolate mixture, then fold that back to the rest of the egg mixture.

Divide this between the prepared pans and level the surface. Bake until risen and just firm to the touch, about 20 minutes. Let cool in the pans, then transfer to wire racks.

Make the filling and decoration: Melt 3 ounces of the chocolate with 6 tablespoons of the cream in a saucepan over very low heat. Beat until smooth, then let cool. Use to sandwich the cake layers together.

Melt 3 ounces of the remaining chocolate with the rest of the cream. Remove from the heat and beat until smooth. Set the cake on a wire rack over a tray and pour the chocolate over the top. Using a metal spatula, spread it over the top and sides to coat the cake completely. Let set.

Melt the remaining chocolate and spread it in a thin layer on a marble or plastic surface. Let set. Using a large knife held at a 45-degree angle to the chocolate and with the blade facing away from you, scrape curls from the chocolate. Set them on a tray and chill until firm.

Use half the marzipan to make miniature mushrooms and dip the tops in cocoa powder. Color half the remaining marzipan with green coloring and the rest with brown. Roll out the green marzipan on a surface lightly dusted with confectioners' sugar or cornstarch. Stamp out small leaves and mark the veins with a knife. Make acorns using the brown marzipan with the green for trimmings.

Arrange the chocolate curls, leaves, acorns, and mushrooms on the surface of the cake and dust with confectioners' sugar.

KITE CAKE

SERVES 16–20

3 sticks (1½ cups) butter, softened, plus more for greasing
1¾ cups sugar
6 eggs, beaten
3 cups self-rising flour (for a chocolate cake replace 6 tbsp flour with 6 tbsp unsweetened cocoa powder and add ⅔ cup chocolate chips)
FOR THE DECORATION
1 recipe Custard Buttercream (see page 57)
½ cup apricot jam, warmed and strained
1 lb 2 oz fondant icing
2 food colorings, such as red and green
two 3-foot lengths of ribbon
confectioners' sugar or cornstarch, for dusting

Preheat the oven to 325°F. Grease a 10-inch square cake pan with butter, then line the bottom with wax or parchment paper.

Cream the butter and sugar until almost white, then beat in the eggs a little at a time until thoroughly incorporated. Fold in the flour (or flour, cocoa powder, and chocolate chips, if using).

Transfer the batter to the prepared pan and level the surface. Bake until risen and just firm to the touch, 1–1¼ hours. Let cool in the pan, then unmold on a wire rack and let cool completely.

Level the surface of the cake if necessary.

To decorate: Cut a 3½-inch rectangular slice off one side of the cake. Cut the remaining large piece in half diagonally.

Cut the rectangular slice to the same length as the shortest sides of the triangles you have just made. Cut that in half diagonally to make 2 smaller triangles. Split each of the 4 triangular pieces of cake into 2 equal layers and sandwich them back together

Top: Kite Cake; bottom: Stopwatch Cake

with some buttercream.

Arrange the 4 filled triangles to form the kite, then stick the pieces together with buttercream. Set on a large tray or silver board and brush the whole surface of the cake with jam.

Cut the fondant icing in half and color each half separately. On a surface lightly sprinkled with confectioners' sugar or cornstarch, roll out one of the pieces of icing thinly and use to cover the tops of diagonally opposite pieces of kite, cutting and fitting as necessary. Repeat with the other color to cover the tops of the remaining two pieces of the kite. Press the icing carefully into position and roll gently with a rolling pin to give a smooth finish.

Re-roll the trimmings and stamp out a message such as "Bon Voyage" or "Happy Birthday" and the name of the celebrant. Cut and attach the ribbon across the seams of icing and pin the rest of the ribbon at the base to represent the tails of the kite.

Dampen the underside of each icing letter and attach to the cake.

STOPWATCH CAKE

SERVES 16–20

2 sticks (1 cup) butter, softened, plus more for greasing
1 ¼ cups sugar
4 tbsp finely grated zest from 1 washed lemon or orange
4 eggs, beaten
2 cups self-rising flour
2 tbsp lemon or orange juice
FOR THE ICING AND DECORATION
1 recipe Custard Buttercream (see page 57)
½ cup sugar sprinkles
about 50 small candies
2-foot length of licorice
small amount of red decorating icing
small amount of black decorating icing
6-inch length of red licorice

Preheat the oven to 325°F. Grease a 10-inch round cake pan with butter, then line the bottom with wax or parchment paper.

Cream the butter and sugar together with the fruit zest until almost white. Beat in the eggs, a little at a time, until thoroughly incorporated. Then fold in the flour and just enough of the fruit juice to give the batter a "soft dropping consistency." Transfer the batter to the prepared pan and level the surface.

Bake until risen and just firm to the touch, about 50 minutes. Let cool slightly, then transfer to a wire rack and let cool completely. Level the surface, if necessary.

To ice and decorate: Spread the buttercream over the top and sides of the cake. Coat the sides and a ring around the outside rim of the top about ¾-inch wide with sugar sprinkles.

Arrange a ring of candies around the top of the cake where the sugar sprinkles finish.

Cut the licorice into four 1-inch, six 2-inch, and two 4-inch pieces. Set out two oblongs measuring 2×1 inch at the top of the cake and use the remaining bits of licorice to make a larger oblong at the bottom. Set a candy above each small oblong to represent the buttons.

Using black icing, pipe the word "start" in the first oblong. Using red icing, pipe the word "stop" in the second oblong. Using red icing, pipe a suitable digital time in the large oblong. Attach a red licorice "strap" to the top of the stopwatch.

Any number of variations on the STOPWATCH CAKE *can be achieved using other candies or edible decorations.*

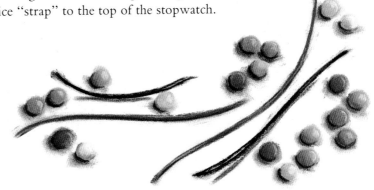

The classic French Croquembouche, meaning literally "crisp in the mouth," is a tall cone of small cream puffs. It is a traditional wedding centerpiece.

CROQUEMBOUCHE COOLER

SERVES 6–8

FOR THE CHOUX PASTRY
3 ½ tbsp butter, plus more for greasing
½ cup + 2 tbsp flour
½ tsp salt
2 eggs

FOR THE FILLING AND DECORATION
2 tbsp cornstarch
1 tbsp flour
2 ⅓ cups sugar
⅔ cup milk
1 egg yolk
2 tbsp Pommeau, Calvados, or applejack
1 cup whipping cream, whipped to soft peaks
⅛ tsp cream of tartar
vegetable oil, for greasing
1 bottle of champagne or sweet wine, for serving

Preheat the oven to 400°F and grease two baking sheets with butter.

Sift the flour and salt together onto a piece of wax paper.

Place the butter in a saucepan with ½ cup water and heat gently until the butter is melted, then bring to a boil. Pour in the flour and beat well to give a thick, smooth paste. Cook gently until the paste leaves the sides of the pan and forms a ball.

Remove from the heat and beat in the eggs, one at a time.

Using a pastry bag fitted with a medium plain tip, pipe 24 mounds of the choux mixture on the baking sheets. With wet fingers, smooth the top of each.

Bake until crisp and golden, about 25 minutes. Then prick each choux puff right through with a skewer and return to the oven for 5 minutes. Let cool on a wire rack.

Make the pastry cream filling: Mix the corn-starch, flour, and 3 tablespoons of the sugar with a little of the milk and the egg yolk to form a paste. Heat the remaining milk in a small saucepan, then pour it on the egg mixture. Mix well, then return to the saucepan and cook over medium heat, stirring, until thickened.

Transfer to a bowl, cover, and let cool. Beat in the alcohol and fold in ⅔ cup of the cream. Chill until required.

Make a hole in the base of each choux puff. Using a pastry bag fitted with a fine tip, fill each one with the chilled pastry cream.

Dissolve half the remaining sugar in sufficient water to cover over very low heat. Add half the cream of tartar and boil to a light caramel.

While the sugar is caramelizing, set a bottle of Champagne or sweet wine on an oiled baking sheet and wrap it with nonstick silicone paper.

When the caramel is ready, remove it from the heat. Holding them with a fork, dip the choux puffs one by one into the caramel and stick them together in a ring around the base of the bottle, with the flat side of each puff toward the bottle. Continue coating the puffs and building up the rings, one layer on top of another. There should be enough caramel to coat a generous half of the puffs.

Make a second batch of caramel with the remaining sugar in the same way, and finish dipping and layering the puffs.

When all the puffs have been dipped and set in position, pour the rest of the caramel on an oiled baking sheet. Let it set, then break in small pieces to represent "crushed ice."

When the choux "cooler" has set hard, remove the bottle and silicone paper and chill both the bottle and the "cooler" separately.

To serve: Set the bottle back in the "cooler" and sprinkle the crushed caramel "ice" over the top.

Fill in any gaps between the puffs by piping rosettes of the remaining whipped cream.

INDEX

ACKNOWLEDGEMENTS

The author, recognizing that producing a book involves great team work, would like to thank everyone who has helped her with this particular book, especially her assistant, Emma Patmore.